NO OPTION BUT NORTH

The Migrant World and the Perilous Path

across the Border

Kelsey Freeman

Photographs by Tess Freeman

PUBLISHING

New York, NY

Copyright © 2020 by Kelsey Freeman.
All rights reserved.

Printed in the United States of America
10 9 8 7 6 5 4 3 2 1

No part of this book may be used or reproduced in any manner without written permission of the publisher. Please direct inquires to:

Ig Publishing
Box 2547
New York, NY 10163

www.igpub.com

ISBN: 978-1-632460-97-4 (paperback)

For Nonna,
who first told me her migration story at bedtime
and who became my unwavering cheerleader.

CONTENTS

Migrants await their next move at *El Refugio*.

María, age three, passes the time at Celaya's long-term shelter, *El Refugio*.

Folkórico dancers gather backstage before a performance in Querétaro.

INTRODUCTION

THE DETAILS WERE ALWAYS OVERWHELMING. I would do my best to take it all in, to feel the emotional force of each story as if it were the very first one I'd ever heard. But in the end, there were no words to describe the grown man crying in front of me, or the many others like him who shared their suffering. His tears—*their* tears—embodied the anguish inflicted upon all those who migrate north, making the choice that really isn't a choice at all.

Back in the United States three years later, I see the same tears in a Mexican-American student as he painfully describes his journey across the Rio Grande. "People just don't get it," he laments as we speak behind a podium after a lecture. It's been over a decade since he crossed, but the trauma of the journey still lives within him. His tears stretch through time and space to join with each grown man that cried in the desert, cried as he said goodbye to his children, cried at the rape of the woman beside him. His tears were the same as all those who said *"Si Dios quiere"* ("God-willing") before attempting the journey for the fifth or sixth time. As he wiped his tears aside and swallowed, he exemplified everyone else before him that buried the hurt and just kept going.

In thinking of all the words to describe the world of migration—a

complex, violent geographic path north from Mexico's southern border to the United States—perhaps the best image is simply tears.

• • •

The author on her daily commute to teach English
at the university where she worked in Celaya.

In January 2016, six months before I would return to Mexico to study
migration, I was traveling in the highlands of Chiapas, winding over
roads that appeared as if they were scribbled atop the mountainous
landscape. This *combi* ride was research for my undergraduate thesis,
which focused on the development of two Indigenous social movements in Latin America (including the Mexican Zapatistas). My thesis explored Indigenous peoples in Mexico who had chosen autonomy
while rejecting the oversight of government systems. Yet in pursuing
this research, I felt a persistent tug in another direction. What about

the many Mayan farmers who had abandoned Mexico altogether? What happened to those who had lost their livelihoods and headed north? It was impossible to separate the study of Indigenous rights from the underlying pull of migration.

During that *combi* (a converted microbus that is part of the public bus system), ride, I sat next to an old man with a large gummy smile and rough *campesino* hands. He alternated fluidly between Tzotzil (a Mayan language) and Spanish as he chatted with his *compañeros*. Eventually he turned to me, sharing a story about how he used to live in Southern California with his family. He recounted the difficulties of living in a foreign place, the exhausting nature of agricultural labor, his frustrating attempt to learn a third language. At least, he sighed, he had been with his family.

Then he spoke of being deported. His sun-kissed wrinkles grew more pronounced as his face scrunched with sorrow. *Desesperación,* he called it. Leaving his family behind some intangible, distant barrier was the essence of despair.

As we approached my destination, my new acquaintance posed a critical question: How was it that I could visit his country to do research for two weeks, when he had been repeatedly rejected for a visa to see his family in my country? It was not a malicious inquiry, nor one intended to induce guilt. He simply wanted to make sense of a system that had blocked his opportunities and separated him from his family, yet still allowed me to casually visit to "study" his people.

This question lingered with me. I knew that being from the United States afforded one enormous privilege. Until that moment in the *combi*, however, I could not start to grasp how thoroughly the cards were stacked against migrants like my traveling companion. His question sparked others: What does it mean to have or lack power while migrating? How do factors like migrants' race, class and nationality affect the legal options available to them? Was my friend on the bus unable to get a visa because he was a poor Indigenous farmer from Mexico?

I became determined to unravel the human element underlying the current state of immigration by examining it, as best I could, from the inside out. In late summer of 2016 (in the thick of the Donald Trump presidential candidacy), I left on a Fulbright grant to teach English at a university and study migration in the industrial city of Celaya, Guanajuato in Central Mexico. Two weeks into my stay, I found the local migrant shelter, became a frequent visitor, and spent much of the next year interviewing the array of travelers who passed through. I also immersed myself in Celaya, a city that lived and breathed migration and was about halfway through the perilous route north.

Like many, I had read countless stories about the human traffickers known as *coyotes* (or *polleros*) and the numerous dangers of crossing the US border. I wanted to delve deeper, however, by exploring the often-cyclical experiences that migrants encounter before they even reach the vast desert that serves as border territory. Meeting migrants in Celaya allowed me to witness the intense weight of the journey—hardships burdening their hunched shoulders and anxieties about the upcoming border coloring their faces.

I choose specifically not to accompany migrants as they headed north, avoiding the sort of immersion journalism that pretends that observing the migration phenomenon doesn't affect it. I am uncomfortable with stories that portray migrant journeys as a form of "extreme" adventure for the writer, one that they inevitably escape with a good-bye and a passport. In my conversations with migrants, I developed a comfort with identifying the power imbalance between us, rather than pretending to be under the same circumstances. While I have included many of my own stories and observations in this book, I have sought to do so in way that serves as a prism into the systemic obstacles in immigration that a white, American woman like myself will never face.

What I found in these migrant stories was far beyond anything I could have possibly anticipated, a dark world deep beneath the surface of life in Mexico filled with kidnapping and assault, cartels and police, rape and unbelievable brutality. A realm where violence and trauma twisted into a harrowing voyage for most migrants, tragically perpetuated by flawed immigration policies on both sides of the border.

Most migrants I spoke to, Central American or Mexican, professed that they were *migrating by necessity*—that walking or riding the train or hitching their way north was their *only* option. At the heart of this frame is the reality that, regardless of how much security sits on the US border, migrants will continue to go north, often more than once, enduring disturbing hazards each time. If migrants know they will face unbelievable suffering and trauma on the journey north, there can be only one reason why they undertake the trek—because there is greater hardship for them at home. Absorbing countless stories of migrants trying to reunite with their families, escaping gang violence, or searching for economic opportunity, I gradually realized that if placed into their situation, I would do exactly the same thing.

If migrants are indeed heading north out of necessity, aren't there *any* legal avenues available to them? Couldn't any of these individuals apply for political asylum or enter on a work visa? A closer look at US immigration policy, however, reveals a broken web of policies that present great systemic barriers for poor Mexicans and Central Americans—and this was even before many of the Trump anti-immigration policies had been enacted. The evidence was overwhelming: when it comes to legal immigration—race, class, and nationality matter.

"*Migrar es sufrir*," many migrants bemoaned as they passed through the migrant shelter in Celaya. *Migrating is suffering.* What *does* it mean to lack power when migrating? The more that I heard these itinerant stories, spilling out in various Spanish dialects, the more it became clear that undertaking this seemingly endless journey north was the essence of political powerlessness.

Although most migrants were only about halfway through the journey when they spoke with me in Celaya, stories of atrocities still resounded. Abraham had been kidnapped by the infamous Zetas, beaten, and barely escaped. Jacqui, an eight-months-pregnant woman traveling with her two toddlers, risked everything whenever she hauled her kids atop the freight train. For them, as for so many I spoke to, poverty at home cruelly turned into helplessness and vulnerability as they headed north. Worse yet, the violence that they were trying to escape only intensified. The result? A harrowing journey that strikes at the heart of the human ability to endure.

During my time in Celaya, I often pondered what it meant to choose to go to another country by choice, as opposed to having to migrate because you had no choice. I was exercising the freedom to live in a new place—those I interviewed decidedly were not. How did this fundamental difference affect the ways in which we were viewed? Throughout the year I spent in Mexico, I observed that my voice often seemed to hold more weight simply because I was white and from the United

States. I was also granted the space to make mistakes and be a foreigner. Meanwhile, in the US, we expect immigrants to know cultural cues, politics, pop culture, English and to grasp the road to economic success. We emphasize assimilation and near-instant contributions. And we allow little room or for error.

This double standard only intensified after the 2016 election of Donald Trump. Vehemently anti-immigrant discourse streamed across the border, juxtaposed against the welcoming way in which I was treated in Mexico. I could not help but reflect on the power dynamics that gave me credibility and a bigger voice in Mexico while further demeaning immigrants in the US.

How does one address the unjust force of the world's contradictions? Ultimately, believe in the power of stories. If we can change the racist narrative aimed at those who cross the southern border, the web of policies that dehumanizes migrants can also shift. This process starts by actually seeing migrants as real people. In retelling their stories, I aim to balance frankness about the disturbing violence many migrants experience with centering their fundamental humanity. The people that I interviewed chose to tell their stories because they wanted to be seen. "Telling you all this makes me lighter," one migrant told me. Ultimately, I came to see that so many migrants—who took significant risk in sharing their stories with a stranger—did so because they wanted you and I to know. They want us to see where their hearts lie.

For those willing to share, I sought to honor their decision by protecting their identities. Many of the names used throughout this book are pseudonyms, and those that are not are typically not full names. I had informal conversations with hundreds of migrants during my time in Celaya, but for the formalized interviews, I either took notes, recorded and transcribed them, or did both, depending on the migrant's preference. Almost all interviews were conducted in Spanish and appear in this book in their translated form, although I have left some words in Spanish to best impart their meaning. While it was not clear in what form these stories would be published at the time of each interview, every migrant who choose to speak to me did so with the knowledge and consent that their stories could be shared in the public domain.

To best serve my goal of capturing their humanity, I included portraits of some of the migrants I interviewed, as well as scenes that depict the complexities of migration. These photos were all shot by photographer (and my sister) Tess Freeman, who collaborated with me on this project during the last six weeks of my time in Mexico. Tess' sensitivity and keen eye for depicting the human spirit and innate beauty behind difficult topics adds layers to this book far beyond what words can accomplish. The people included in these photos supported their use, appreciating that they might provide insight and perspective that readers might not otherwise see.

While I sometime use the word "powerless" to describe migrants, I do not want to suggest that migrants lack agency or dignity. On the contrary, migrants develop complicated systems to navigate violent forces on their path north—whether by passing information down in whispers, or traveling in caravans thousands of people strong. Rather, when I speak of the them as "powerless" I am referring to the fact that they exist in a vulnerable political state where US and Mexican political and public discourse push their stories to the margins and portray the violence they face as simply a natural consequence of their "decision" to cross the border illegally.

This book is ultimately about respect for those that overcome the systemic obstacles. It highlights that migration is a game of options, or lack thereof. Those of certain races, nationalities and class are more likely to leave their country but are less likely to have legal avenues for migrating. They then put themselves at extraordinary risk to climb the ladder toward safety and prosperity. In short, a lack of privileges leads to a lack of options, which in turn creates an incredibly vulnerable population repeatedly traveling through Mexico and across the border.

In speaking with dozens of migrants, one thing was astoundingly clear: migration will not cease. Not with an increase of border security, the shifting of border crossing points to remote sections of the Sonoran desert, the building of an "impenetrable" wall, or the separation of families. Instead, migrants will continue to risk everything because their alternate options for survival and decency have run out. The many stories included in this book are certainly not the most horrifying tales that come out of the journey north. Instead, they serve as a first-hand, humanist account of the varying experiences faced by those who head for *el norte*. And it is my hope that they stand testament not only to the senseless pain that structural violence has inflicted on them, but also the fundamental dignity interlaced in all that they endure.

PART ONE

POR NECESIDAD

"Many don't know where they are going, but they know what they're leaving behind."

> —Miroslava Cerpas, in regard to the second migrant caravan, Center for Research and Promotion of Human Rights in Tegulchigalpa.[1]

One

DIVIDED BY LAW

THROUGH THE VISCOUS FOG OF a December dawn, headlights divided the darkness. Beside me, Roberto looked expectant, seasoned, practiced. His body a silhouette, shadows dirty across his cheeks, he prepared for what he had done a hundred times before. The metallic beast roared. In seconds he would be gone.

"*¿Todo bien?*" I managed haltingly—a stupid question, but the quiet murmurs of the other migrants around us overwhelmed me. My hands hung impossibly heavy at my sides.

"*Todo bien,*" he confirmed. And then the headlights were upon us, interrupting the swath of shadows. "*Nos vemos,*" Roberto called out as he took off running. The others did the same. Soon there were dozens of men galloping ahead, trying to catch the *La bestia* (the beast) as the migrants called it. Their rhythm gathered steam as they attempted to time their gait to the relentless pounding of the giant wheels. They all knew that if a hand slipped, or never quite grasped the rungs, their stories would end with their flesh shredded on the jagged teeth of the tracks.

Roberto and the others melted into the fog ahead. The grumbling train became a blurry film in my periphery as I observed their images disappearing into the darkness. I imagined each one jumping, then crawling up the sides of the beast like little spiders. But I didn't really know.

"*Nos vemos*," I whispered. *See you later*. But I never really expected to see any of them again.

The tracks.

The Love of Your Life

I rarely ventured to the train tracks, preferring instead to conduct my migrant interviews at the shelter. I would walk the twenty minutes to the *albergue, casa de migrante, refugio*, where, upon entering, the black metallic door would slam behind me like a cleaver. *You again?* Lupita, the main shelter employee, would frequently say, shooting me an indifferent look. Rambunctious curls dominated her hoggish head, and I wondered if she ever smiled. After wordlessly signing me in, she would return to her computer outpost to shamelessly take selfies from every conceivable angle, then post each one to Facebook.

The migrants would gather in the adjacent mudroom by the door.

Fraying couches fringed the room, the upholstery peeling off like dried skin. The floor was dirt with gravel strewn haphazardly; random sheets of fake grass posed as carpeting. Cracks formed labyrinths in the white walls, and two lone light bulbs poked through the ceiling, their wires braided like vines. Since Geoff (the director of the shelter) was never present and Lupita was always preoccupied, I would have to introduce myself to the newest group of migrants. They would be draped across the couches, tired enough to seem boneless. They wore jeans and torn jackets, baseball caps and shoes with floppy soles. A few slunk off into the corners as we gathered, but most accepted my invitation to join the conversation. They wanted to tell their stories.

Martín, José, and I formed a seated triangle in the living room. Martín was trying to return to his family in the US, while José had just left his behind in Honduras. Martín spoke frequently; he was the type to let his words roll on until you couldn't remember the epicenter of his original point. He flooded me with a river of stories that carved their own channels rather than following any logical progression. A black baseball cap covered his shaved head, and a hefty wooden cross hung just below his sternum. The cross swung from side to side in a rhythm that seemed to accompany his words.

He had first migrated to the United States from El Salvador with his mother and grandmother when he was eleven years old. While it was difficult to tell which stories were his and which he had merely encountered during his years in the migration labyrinth, one thing was clear: his daughter was his life and therefore his life was in the United States. "Sometimes I dream that I'm holding my daughter just for ten minutes. Ten minutes is all I need to feel alive again."

Martín had been deported from the United States eight years ago. He did not try to return immediately. Rather, he spent several years working in Honduras and Mexico while applying for legal avenues to enter the US. However, since he never qualified for a visa, when Martín lost his job in San Luis Potosí, Mexico, he decided to try to enter the US illegally. Years had passed since he had seen his daughter. He wasn't prepared to wait any longer. "Just hearing from my family is a way to help me keep going," he reflected. "It's like charging up my battery." His hunched shoulders and crumpled brow revealed how it tore at him to be apart from his daughter. "We would talk on the phone and she would say to me 'Daddy, are you gonna come back?' And I would say, 'Soon, *Mija*. I really hope soon.'"

As Martín journeyed down another tunnel of his life story, my mind began to drift to the last time I had seen my family. Just four months earlier. I replayed the moment—a drive to the airport that hung clearly in the clouds of my memories. We had already said everything we needed to say about my leaving for Mexico, how it was a great opportunity, how they'd visit. So, with nothing left unspoken, we blasted Taylor Swift's first album, a favorite of my fifty-six-year-old father. We zanily bobbed our heads back and forth as we belted out Taylor's lyrics, dramatizing the lovesick nature of the songs with over-the-top facial expressions. Nothing is quite as funny as listening to your dad make his voice as high as it can go and passionately sing, "I can't help it if you look like an angel, can't help it if I wanna kiss you in the rain, so." As we passed by the road sign marking ten miles until the airport, however, my laughter gradually turned to crying. The dichotomy between the fullness of my family and venturing out into new terrain fully hit home as I unloaded my bags, had one final hug, and headed toward the check-in line.

José listened from the corner of our triangle, adding his thoughts infrequently. Yet when he did share something, he seemed to be putting new meaning to his circumstances with each word he uttered. "My daughter asked me once, 'Daddy, are we poor?' And I said, 'Yes we are.' And because of that, I'm in the situation I'm in . . . We lived in the rough part of town and when you live like that, you survive by your fingernails. I've seen my kids cry because they were hungry. So I had to leave. I didn't have any other option. I couldn't stay and do nothing." José then began to describe the paradox that is leaving your family out of love for them. The urge to provide, to see his children flourish, overpowered his yearning to stay with them.

"A few months ago, I was talking to my mom on the phone," Martín interjected. "And you know what she said to me? She said 'I've never said I love you. I've helped you, I've taken care of you, but I want you to know that I love you.'" A softness hung in the air. "And to know that my mom loves me, well it changed my life. It filled me up."

Later that night, rereading letters from my family, I felt this tangle of emotions. Part of it was the longing for my family, that space of wholeness and comfort. But laced within that familiar feeling was the knowledge that I would see them when they visited, very soon, while so many others who loved their families just as much as I did, like Martín and José, did not know when—or if—they would ever see their families again. The weight of that thought made me feel as if something was pulling my limbs in opposite directions, contorting my body with the potency of the world's contradictions.

I recalled a moment that José had shared earlier in the shelter. He and his daughter used to play a little game. "(My daughter) would say, 'Papi, Papi, who am I?'" he'd said, "and I would always answer, 'Mija, you're the love of my life.'"

Like Martín and José, the majority of migrants I interviewed in Celaya were either leaving their families back in their home country or seeking to reunite with them in the States. These migrants were typically men in their twenties or thirties. Because the pressure to provide is gendered in most Latin American countries, men with no viable means of financially supporting their families confront a potent sense of inadequacy. This leads to what anthropologist Jason De León describes as "the experience of being caught between the pull of a semi-living wage working in the often exploitative US undocumented labor force and the shame of returning to Mexico penniless," which he notes "is common for many male Mexican migrants."[1] This tension also exists for Central American migrants like José, who displayed his shame as he dejectedly stared at the floor when describing his family's economic state. Men like José are willing to put their lives on the line and leave their families for even the chance to work the lowest paying jobs under the worst conditions in America. Many described to me how difficult it was to say goodbye; some avoided the process altogether and just left. All noted that their plan was to remain in the US for two to three years, send money back to their family, and then return home. Many showed me pictures of the families they'd left behind—faded bits of visual memory as worn down by the journey as the people carrying them.

As was the case with Martín, migrants who were going to reunite with their families often already had very established lives in the States. Some had even raised children who were US citizens. As immigration reform increasingly focuses on deporting non-criminal immigrants, however, more and more families continue to be separated. In 2017, Immigration and Customs Enforcement (ICE) deported 27,080 undocumented immigrants who claimed at least one US citizen child, according to two Department of Homeland Security (DHS) reports.[2] These are over 27,000 individuals who are unlikely to accept being apart from their families, their lives. Instead, they are likely to head north again, perpetuating a cyclical migration that is almost impossible to deter.

While under the Obama administration ICE claimed to focus its resources on apprehending violent criminals and gang members, in reality, many who faced deportation had committed minor, nonviolent crimes, or had no criminal record at all. A study conducted by the Transactional Records Access Clearinghouse (TRAC) found that in 2013, "two categories that ICE has classified as convicted criminals—namely those with a traffic violation and individuals convicted of immigration offenses—comprised half of all those classified by ICE as criminal deportees."[3] In other words, "criminal" included a wide variety of offenses—from traffic violations to simply having entered the country illegally.

Under the Trump administration, ICE has shifted its priorities even further away from targeting violent criminals. In his 2016 campaign for president, Donald Trump famously pushed the idea that there were "bad hombres" out there that he would prioritize for apprehension.[4] However, during the first year of his presidency, ICE arrested 109,000 criminals and 46,000 people without criminal records, a 171 percent increase of non-criminal arrests compared to 2016.[5] Additionally, by the end of 2018, the overall number of individuals in ICE custody had increased by 22 percent from 2016, but the number of those who had committed serious crimes had fallen by 17 percent.[6] In fact, 82 percent of immigrants in ICE custody by the end of 2018 either had no conviction or had committed a minor offense, such as a traffic violation.[7] This increase in non-criminal apprehensions has been one of defining features of Trump's approach to immigration.

The growth in non-criminal apprehensions was made possible by the Executive Order on Interior Enforcement, which Trump signed on January 27, 2017. Section 5 of the executive order dramatically expanded the list of noncitizens subject to deportation, including those that:

> Have been convicted of any criminal offense; have been charged with any criminal offense, where such charge has not been resolved; have committed acts that constitute a chargeable criminal offense; have engaged in fraud or willful misrepresentation in connection with any official matter or application before a governmental agency; have abused any program related to receipt of public benefits; are subject to a final order of removal, but who have not complied with their legal obligation to depart the United States; or in the judgment of an immigration officer, otherwise pose a risk to public safety or national security.[8]

There are several key ways that this order expanded ICE's ability to apprehend non-criminals. First, there is no clarification as to which of these categories should be prioritized. In addition, the order includes those that are suspected of, but have not necessarily been convicted of, crimes, expanding the list of immigrants who can be targeted. Third, explicitly including those engaging in "willful misrepresentation" means that many undocumented immigrants who falsify papers to work can be targeted for deportation. When there is almost no path to legal residency for those who already have established lives in the US, misrepresenting one's status to work becomes a crucial way to make a living. Lastly, deciding who poses "a threat to public safety" is left to the whims of the immigration officer, which suggests that there is no supervisory review and opens the door to racial profiling. With this broad legal platform for deportation, the mother who falsified her legal status to provide for her family is as much of a priority as the gang member.

When those who already have lives and families in the US are deported, they do not simply accept it. Instead, most turn around and go right back, a fact the government tends to ignore. They simply have too much at stake not to at least try, as their children and husbands and wives and parents are just a border away. In addition, they have work and economic security in the US, and their home countries may have become unfamiliar after they have spent decades living in the States. Thus, we do not solve anything by separating families. Rather, we create more anguish for our US citizen children and more obstacles for their undeterred parents to overcome to get back to them.

Alejandro was one such migrant trying to jump the hurdles to get back to his family.

The Silences that Hang in Hard Truths

"I do whatever I can to see my baby." Alejandro repeated several iterations of this sentence during our conversation. His wife and four-year-old daughter lived in Texas. Alejandro had previously migrated to the US as an adolescent, living in Texas for twelve years before he was deported in April 2016. A policeman pulled him over for a minor traffic violation, brought him into the police station when he couldn't show identification, and detained him when it was confirmed that he was undocumented. Alejandro tried to qualify for Deferred Action for Childhood Arrivals (DACA), an Obama-era program launched in 2012 that offered certain migrants who had arrived in the US before they turned sixteen a work permit, as well as protection from deportation, but he was rejected. (Although the Trump Administration terminated the program in 2017, after a series of lawsuits, those who had or previously had DACA status were allowed to continue to renew it. However, new DACA applications are no longer being accepted, and of this writing, it appears likely that the Supreme Court will permanently allow the program to end.)

During the lead-up to his deportation, Alejandro spent hours signing paperwork, but was only allowed three minutes to speak to his family. He returned to Honduras, his home country, only to immediately begin planning to return to the US. "I spent twelve years there," he said defiantly. "That's my life. If you get me, I just come back. I'd try twenty, fifty times so that I can be with my baby."

My interview with Alejandro had begun as part of a larger conversation with a group of about twenty-five migrants. I hovered on the edge of a couch as I explained my purpose for being at the shelter. I was writing a book and wanted to talk to those who wanted to tell me their story. Then, as Geoff, the director of the migrant shelter, had requested, I tentatively launched into a planned discussion about cultural differences in America. Yet as my questions sat on a clipboard in my lap, I realized how irrelevant they were. Who cared about differences across the border when the real concern was just getting there? Abandoning my talking points, I let the conversation flow wherever it needed to go. Like an open mic night at a dark café, the stage went from story to silence, story to silence.

Alejandro was the first one to speak, answering my questions in clear accented English. He began by describing the importance of his family, who were the source of his motivation for migrating. But once he made it clear why he was migrating, he shifted to describing the destitute journey north. "You can be scared. From everything," he observed, crossing his legs and squeezing them together. He stooped over his knees, his back like the crooked ficus tree that sprouted out of a pot in the corner.

He started with *la bestia,* the infamous freight train that had been his transportation for his previous trip to the border, which he would now rely on again. He described the terrifying practice of running full speed at a freight train moving thirty or more miles per hour while trying to pull yourself on top. Once aboard, Alejandro had to immediately survey his surroundings, looking out for thieves and bandits. "Every time I ride the train, I got like twenty rocks with me," he told me in a guarded tone. "I'll hit them. I don't have nothing to lose. I've got to protect my life." He also said that some people slept on top of the train, but that he always refrained from doing so, not just to be vigilant of thieves and bandits, but also because he knew people who had fallen off the train when it stopped or rounded a sharp bend.

Despite the risks of the train, Alejandro maintained that, "I feel better in the train because if *la migra* (a generalized term that migrants use for the immigration patrol, whether it be Mexican immigration forces or the US Border Patrol) comes, you can run." He compared this to taking the bus, where, if it is stopped at a checkpoint, Central Americans have to either bribe the officials or face deportation. Alejandro's preference for the dangers of the train over risking an encounter with the border patrol highlights how increased surveillance and security merely lead migrants to take on greater hardships to avoid getting caught.

Alejandro was unsure about the options that remained ahead for him. He absentmindedly picked at his sandal as he estimated the time it would take to get to the border—four more days on the train to

Monterey, the capital city of Nuevo León. From there, he would have to hire a *pollero*. Alejandro was hoping that his family would recommend someone who was trustworthy. Otherwise, he explained, you might end up with a person who takes your money and then either abandons you in the desert, assaults you, kidnaps you for ransom, or makes you smuggle drugs. "It used to be that you could find—I think they're called *cowboys*," he added, chuckling as he rolled the strangeness of the word through his mouth. "They used to help you. Now they stick a gun to you." He looked up at me for the first time in our conversation and shook his head, followed by a momentary silence.

"They treat you like slobs here," Alejandro declared, moving on to a new subject. He shot a dirty look at Lupita, who was on Facebook, as usual. Indeed, the shelter was very strict about what migrants could and could not do. They had to stay in the entryway until dinner. They were only allowed short intervals for eating, showering, and sleeping. All their actions were closely scrutinized. At the time, I attributed these rules to the shelter's standard security measures. Over the following weeks and months, however, as my Facebook messages to Alejandro went unanswered, I initially feared that the perils of the journey north might have ensnared him. Eventually, as I dug deeper and deeper into the corrupt and haunted world of migration—and learned what was happening behind the scenes at the shelter—I wondered if Alejandro had even made it out of Celaya.

Before he left to eat dinner, I asked Alejandro what message he would convey to Americans who denounced immigrants. He shot me a quizzical look. What would he say to Donald Trump? "Well, I have a lot to tell Trump." He let out a sound halfway between a chortle and a snort before answering, "You think you can cut the grass and do all we do?" He pointed out how Trump relied on the work of immigrants for his businesses. Then he paused for a moment. "No, I know what I'd tell Trump. I'd ask if he could live separately from his family. What would he do?"

Two

LA VIOLENCIA

"SOMETIMES HAVING THE CARTEL AROUND is better than the police."

My student swerved between lanes as he spoke, in hectic rhythm with the darting cars ahead. "Teacher, you want a ride," he had offered as I was waiting at the bus stop. I crawled into his Hyundai and sat upright in the passenger seat, trying to focus on our conversation as I covertly gripped the door handle.

Our discussion had turned to Querétaro, the nearest big city to Celaya and one of the safest metropolises in Mexico. I had just spent a Friday night there with a Fulbright friend, and as we roamed the downtown streets at 11:00 PM, I could feel the difference in terms of security between the city and other ones I had visited in Mexico. Querétaro is a classic colonial capital, with a picturesque downtown filled with statues, cozy gardens, and the elegant and ornate architecture of earlier centuries. It was a place that my friend (also a young woman) and I could walk around freely and securely, even at night. Why was Querétaro so safe, when just an hour west in Celaya, police were being assassinated in broad daylight? The rumor was that several cartel leaders lived in Querétaro, and naturally wanted to keep the foulness of the drug trade out of their own backyards. They didn't shit where they ate, so to speak.

As I dug deeper into migration from Mexico, it became impossible to ignore the role that organized crime played in so many people's decision to leave. The connection is simple: when crime networks pay off local police to turn the other cheek; bribe politicians to work with them (and assassinate those who don't); use the media to glorify their murders and induce fear; and kill thousands of civilians in the crossfire, there is little wonder why so many people flee.

Yet cartels were not always so intertwined with the essential functions of the Mexican state. When these organized crime units were simply decentralized networks of drug smugglers, innocent Mexican civilians could largely avoid their brutality. However, as corruption and lack of economic opportunity festered, these smugglers evolved into highly organized killing operations that, in many states in Mexico, usurped the powers of the government. In the places where they maintain control, it is nearly impossible for the average person not to be touched by the presence of the cartels.

While in many circumstances, cartels force civilians into their world, in other cases—particularly in areas where there is little economic opportunity—people choose to join them. Ioan Grillo, a British journalist who has done extensive research on cartel violence in Mexico describes how, in Ciudad Juárez, assassins hired by the Juárez Cartel (many of whom are teenage boys) are paid just 1,000 pesos to murder someone. As Grillo puts it, "For someone to take a life for just $85— enough to eat some tacos and buy a few beers over the week—shows a terrifying degradation in society."[1] However, with so little economic opportunity in many border towns and rural areas, the drug cartels often offer the only viable means of employment, as well as a grossly skewed type of empowerment for the malleable teenage minds they frequently capture.

After my Friday night in posh Querétaro, I headed to a village in the mountains of Hidalgo to visit another friend. Accessing the village required a two-hour taxi ride from the nearest city. As we wound our way over pothole-filled country roads, we crossed over from the dry, cactus-speckled hills of Tulancingo into a lush temperate forest. Mountains turned from rounded lumps to precipitous ridges, and the pieces of me that had been sanded down by Celaya's industrial drudgery felt alive again in the remoteness. It was dark, but I could still trace the outline of the cliffs above, partially illuminated by a globular moon.

La bestia passes through Querétaro.

In the morning, as clumps of fog clustered at the tops of the mountains, I realized that the village was located in a bowl with a rim of green cliffs in every direction. Though my friend's concrete house had little boxy rooms, a bucket-flush toilet, a cow grazing outside, and limited running water, it felt cozy tucked in the greenery of the *pueblito*. Such small Mexican towns possess something that can only be described as magical. There's an undeniable sense of community, evident in the teenage schoolgirls that rove the streets in tight *V*s to snicker and gossip, and the old *señor* who leads his ox toward the main square. The woman making tortillas on the corner emanates a maternal warmth as she offers a piping hot sample. The town's cadence is melodic, and everyone knows your parents, your *abuelos*, your *bisabuelos*. Even the outsider feels at home.

That evening, we attended someone's *Quinceañera*, and the whole town seemed to be crowded around the birthday girl as she received her crown in the local gymnasium. Even though I stood out horribly (and thus could not pretend I was invited), I peeked in on the party behind a line of men in black cowboy hats, extending onto my tiptoes to see. "Over here," a stranger remarked, ushering me toward the front where I could better view the preteen in her sumptuous outfit. Invited or not, I was a guest now.

Later that night, we went to another party, the sixtieth birthday of a friend of a friend. This party was certainly more intimate than the giant *Quinceñera*, with about ten people gathered in a little room to eat *mole* and *barbacoa* and *gorditas* and cake. To my delight, the cakes by far outnumbered the people.

"The thing is that people have to feed themselves," a friend of a friend of a new friend offered. We were in the corner of the party, a full cake on the table between us. He had grown up in the village and witnessed his family members and friends struggle to find any kind of decent job. Many did the four-hour round-trip commute to Tulancingo for work, paying the 100 pesos for a shared taxi each way, a significant chunk out of a meager paycheck. Others worked in the fields and tried to sustain themselves in a market that was increasingly turning to cheap, processed food imported from the US. And then there were those that realized that in a largely decrepit local economy, it was easier to make a quick buck from the cartel than to toil away looking for work. "When you come from a tiny rural town and there's no other options," my new friend continued, "the cartel can say 'hey, want to make some money,' and you basically have to say yes. You have to make money somehow. So that's why the cartel is kind of like a hero in some places." Indeed, in many poor areas of Mexico, drug capos are revered rather than feared, since, to many, they epitomize a kind of rags-to-riches success story. To build up this heroic image, capos such as the notorious El Chapo Guzmán have taken on a government-like role in their home states, paving roads, providing jobs, and helping "protect" people from outside kidnappers and extortionists. For those that have struggled their whole lives for any measure of financial stability, the cartel represents an opportunity to finally advance. At the same time, becoming involved in the drug trade only provides a tenuous sense of stability, since once you're in, you're forced to comply, or face death.

There were layers to this town tucked in the mountains, and other towns like it. Community and closeness, mountains and tranquil beauty were subtly interspersed with isolation, eroding economic opportunity and the dangers it bred. With each town that I explored in Mexico, I tried to balance two notions—the inaccurate stereotype of Mexico as unsafe and crime ridden with the reality that unquestionable dangers do exist for the residents that bear the brunt of organized crime. When morbid violence strangles local life, ordinary citizens have a choice: they can grab a gun, shut themselves into their homes, or flee north.

After that conversation in Hidalgo, I began to wonder what fueled the power of the cartels. Lack of economic opportunity is one factor, of course, but that doesn't explain the level of brutality that plague parts of the country. How did these cartels come to be? And how did they evolve from relatively benign black market businesses to covertly control several Mexican states?

The burliest of the cartels, Sinaloa and Los Zetas, grew as most large businesses do: by rapid expansion, consuming smaller organizations, and enlarging their territory to monopolize the industry. The obvious difference, however, is that corporations do not murder scores of people in order to achieve their growth, nor do they control everyday citizens by infusing the public with fear.

Take the Zetas, for instance, the cartel that sprouted from the Nuevo Laredo region into a highly militarized apparatus with no regard for human life. The corridor up through Texas had long been an area for transporting drugs. In 1997, however, when drug lord Osiel Cárdenas Guillén begun to earn his nickname *"Mata Amigos"* (friend killer), the Nuevo Laredo region was about to see a new influx of brutality and violence that would change the nature of the cartel world. Shortly after Cárdenas Guillén gained his reputation as someone to be intensely feared through the Gulf Cartel, he befriended Arturo Guzmán Decena (not to be confused with El Chapo Gúzman of the Sinaloa Cartel). Guzmán Decena was a lieutenant with the *Grupo Aeromóvil de Fuerzas Especiales,* a Special Forces unit in the Mexican army that had been trained in counter insurgency and urban warfare by American, Israeli, and French authorities, with the specific aim of clamping down on the cartels. As was not uncommon, Guzmán Decena and Cárdenas

Guillén's relationship began when Cárdenas Guillén bribed the lieutenant to ignore drug-related activity and murders. While bribing officials has long been rampant in Mexico, the idea that a military commander could defect to actually *join* a cartel was unprecedented. That, however, is exactly what occurred as Guzmán Decena went from bystander to accomplice in the rise of the Zetas.[2]

Although it is not entirely clear what caused Guzmán Decena to defect, the lure of earning sums unimaginable in the military likely had a lot to do with it. Once Guzmán Decena joined Cárdenas Guillén, he began actively recruiting other soldiers and police officers. Over the course of just a few months, the newly formed Zetas grew to thirty-eight former soldiers. Each was given a Z code name according to their rank, with Guzmán Decena heading the squadron as Z-1. As the operation later expanded, the Zetas took to advertising for new recruits; some of their ads were written on blankets that they hung over bridges. One such blanket read, "The Zetas operations wants you, soldier or ex-soldier. We offer you a good salary, food, and attention for your family. Don't suffer hunger and abuse anymore."[3] As the Zetas' name became synonymous with power, frustrated soldiers seeking clout continued to defect to them.

Many of the violent tactics rampant in the Mexican military in the 1990s gained a flagrant level of brutality with the Zetas, and by the early 2000s, both Cárdenas Guillén and Guzmán Decena had made it to the top of Mexico's hit list. In 2002, Mexican troops stormed a restaurant where Guzmán Decena was eating and shot him; the following year, Cárdenas Guillén was arrested. Theoretically, chopping off the heads of the Zeta monster should have killed it. However, as has been the case with many cartels in Mexico, killing the capos did nothing to quell the violent forces already at work, nor did it discourage the numerous men eager to join. Additionally, when one cartel falters, it only helps rival groups. Such proved to be the case with the Zeta capos.

With Cárdenas Guillén and Guzmán Decena out of the picture, the rival Sinaloa Cartel jumped on the opportunity to expand its territory. Sinaloa already monopolized the border section from Juaréz to the Pacific Ocean, but seized the chance to now control the entire border. As Sinaloan drug lords moved into Zeta territory, they began taxing Zeta dealers and drug smugglers. Some of these low-level employees welcomed this new force, hoping that they would be more generous employers than the Zetas. The rest of the Zeta squadron, however, fought back, employing tactics that would up the ante for cartel violence in Mexico. In 2004, the Zetas left five mutilated Sinaloan cadavers in a Nuevo Laredo safe house with a note that read, "Chapo Guzmán and Beltrán Leyva (capos) send more *pendejos* like this for us to kill."[4] The violence continued to escalate as the Sinaloa-Zeta turf war spread to other regions in Mexico. In 2005, there were 1,500 cartel-related murders across Mexico. The following year, that number had surged to 2,000. Mexico's first major turf war had begun.

On a March evening in Celaya, I was walking the streets holding a tray of mini cream donuts. My friend Otty pulled a cart behind her with numerous platters of the doughy balls of fat. Our initial clientele had been the children pouring out of the local elementary school at the end of their day, but since we still had leftovers after the kids dispersed, we wandered the *taquerías* to offer our supply. Both Otty and her brother Uzziel were professors, but since even academics are paid very little in Mexico, Otty sold donuts on the side to help her family make ends meet. "Can you sell things like this in the US?" she asked as she guided the cart over the sidewalk bumps, cracks and holes. A Coca-Cola sign lit up the taco shop behind her.

"Not quite like this," I replied, smirking at how little each restaurant seemed to care about us selling our own food at their establishment.

The gunshots didn't even register when I first heard them.

"I think there was a shooting," Otty stated nonchalantly, as we tee-tered on the curb outside a taco joint. Somehow, I misunderstood or didn't hear her. Otty, obviously accustomed to the distant ring of gun-shots, and I, completely oblivious to what had just happened, carried on with our enterprise as if everything was normal.

We noticed the exodus of people fleeing the street corner only after they surrounded us. "You shouldn't go any further," a woman called out, pausing briefly before being swept away with the flow of the crowd. "*Hubo una balacera,*" she added in her wake. *There was a shootout.*

"Oh," Otty shrugged. "I guess I was right." We immediately turned around and headed back toward home.

Shootouts, murders, and kidnappings were common occurrences when I was in Celaya. And while it was difficult to know which crimes were cartel-related, I suspected that many, if not most of them, were. During my eight months in the city, I heard endless rumors about the drug trade. *"Todo está bien si no te metes en problemas,"* was a frequent warning. *As long as you aren't involved with the drug trade in any way, you'll be fine.* Which seemed largely true. But *"meterse en problemas"* or *getting into trouble* could affect even those who were not involved in illicit activities. Since Celaya is located just north of Michoacán, a state the cartels have all but taken over, it was said to be a strategic center for drug distribution. A few years before I arrived, two rival cartels had battled for control of the city. Not unlike the Sinaloa-Zeta turf war, the battle over Celaya had left many civilians dead in its wake.

Eventually, after a period where the murder rates in Celaya soared and citizens became afraid to leave their houses at night, one cartel appeared to win out. As is common in many towns in Mexico, the mayor was rumored to have made a deal with the winning cartel: stop killing civilians in Celaya and the city will look the other way on your drug operations. While a municipality working with a cartel is far from ideal, there are often few other options to quell the violence. The cartel that was rumored to take root in Celaya following the deal was named La Familia Michoacana, an organization that combined its criminal activities with a fanatic religious ideology.

La Familia Michoacana first emerged out of the rural town of Tierra Caliente in Michoacán, and gained international attention with its stunning acts of violence, such as rolling five severed heads across the floor of a nightclub in 2006. A sign left along with the heads read, "La Familia doesn't kill for money. It doesn't kill women; it doesn't kill innocent people—only those who deserve to die. Everyone should know: this is divine justice."[5] The cultish cartel was originally allied with the Zetas and Gulf Cartel, but once it had trained enough gangsters using the Zeta's military-style brutality, it flipped and began to kill Zetas and Gulf Cartel members to gain control over their territory—an area that began in Michoacán, but later would extend into Guanajuato, Jalisco, Guerrero, Puebla, and Estado de Mexico.

La Familia capos all hailed from rural Tierra Caliente, and portrayed themselves as humble, poor heroes, and defenders of their region. Unlike other cartels, they also imbedded their killing and extortion with religious zeal. Narzio Moreno González, one of the three capos of the cartel, took on the role of religious indoctrinator, eventually dispensing his own bible of sorts entitled *Pensamientos* or "Thoughts." The book literally jumps from thought to thought, preaching an alluring ideology about "defending ideas" and "building consciousness." One particular passage proclaims, "It is better to be a master of one peso than a slave of two; it is better to die fighting head-on than on your knees and humiliated."[6] This rhetoric of course ignores the fact that if you work for the cartel, you are largely a slave to your superiors and are hardly fighting for the greater good. Nevertheless, the message still caught on with the many *michoacanos* who viewed this cartel as a welcome alternative to a corrupt police force and government.

To further draw people into their "cause," La Familia capos targeted the vulnerable with protection and services. According to one informant, La Familia members would visit rehab centers, hospitals, employment offices and migrant shelters across the state to target those in desperate circumstances. They would provide these individuals with clothing, shelter, food, rehab and prayer meetings, with the understanding that they would then become cartel employees.[7] La Familia also characterized itself as a regional "protector," shielding people from outside extortionists and kidnappers. In one publicity stunt, the group rounded up several alleged kidnappers and rapists in the town of Zamora, killing five and publicly berating the rest.[8] Such acts succeeded in winning over some supporters who argued that La Familia was better at ensuring that justice was served than Mexico's judicial system. Others, however, pointed out that while the cartel may have killed some supposed criminals, they went on to extort and kidnap in their place.

When Nazario Moreno González died in 2010, La Familia began to splinter and reorganize. The following year, banners appeared across Michoacán announcing the formation of a new cartel: Los Caballeros Templarios. While it was a mystery as to who specifically led the new cartel, they were still one of the main forces behind the trafficking of marijuana, meth, and heroin in Michoacán, Guanajuato and other states.

Thus, it was unclear exactly who exactly controlled Celaya when I first set foot in the city in 2016. What was clear, however, was that cartel violence dramatically affected people's lives. It affected how safe they felt walking outside at night, and how worried they were about their children being kidnapped. And it affected whether or not someone might make the choice to leave the country.

Don't Leave Rocks on the Pavement

A few weeks before Christmas 2016, my family came to visit. It was liberating to share my Mexican "outsiderness" with them, the ultimate insiders in my life. My sister, Tess, arrived in Mexico City after my parents, and my father and I drove through the twisting vehicular pipelines of one of the world's biggest cities to pick her up. After accidentally directing my father the wrong way down a busy one-way street, barely skirting a head-on collision, and talking our way out of arrest, we grabbed my sister and bee-lined it out of the city.

It was the evening of December 12, the day of the Virgen de Guadalupe. To celebrate, thousands of Mexicans set off on a pilgrimage each year to the Basilica in Mexico City. Day and night, they carry torches and walk, run, bike, or crowd in every type of vehicle known to man to get there. The cars that surround the pilgrims are adorned with flashing lights and pictures of La Virgen. Thousands embark on their pilgrimages via the highway—meaning that you might be driving along at eight-five kilometers per hour, only to have to slam on the breaks to avoid plowing into a large group of pedestrians in the middle of the road. As we rounded our way toward the mountains in Veracruz, we encountered dozens of these groups.

During their visit, my family would joke about the numerous highway signs that read *No dejes piedras sobre el pavimento. Don't leave rocks on the pavement.* My rock-loving father has never left a place without bringing home an assortment of stones, and on this particular occasion, he was hauling around a fifteen-pound boulder in the trunk that I had lugged down from the 18,700 foot Pico de Orizaba for him. (Only later did we learn that you are not supposed to extract natural objects from the peak.) My sister and I decided that this sign was directed toward our father, a warning of sorts for his illicit activity. "Don't leave your stolen rocks here, Dad." We repeated versions of this joke endlessly, our father finding it less hilarious each time.

A week later, on a family excursion in a taxi, my sister casually asked the driver about the "rocks on the pavement" signs. "Well, it's gotten better, but this area used to be pretty unsafe," Carlos, the driver began. "There were a lot of demonstrations and people would make road blockades with rocks to protest." I had been stuck behind a few different blockades in Chiapas myself, one of which required leaving our bus and continuing on in the back of a pick-up. "But in this area, even more than road blockades, people would throw rocks on the pavement as a form of assault."

"Assault?"

"Yeah, organized crime was pretty bad around here."

I was glad that my mother in the back seat wasn't following our conversation. "What changed?" I inquired.

"Well, basically the municipal government made some sort of deal with the cartel. You know, stop killing civilians and we'll let you exist." At that point during my time in Mexico, I hadn't yet encountered any *narco-related* activity up close—my Celaya consisted of a university, *taquerias*, cafes, and a dance class.

"So does the cartel still affect this area? Do you see their presence?"

"Well, yeah. The taxi drivers see them plenty. They charge us a quota just for operating. And if you don't pay, then there's trouble." I had heard this same story from the Honduran and Salvadorian migrants that came through the shelter in Celaya—if you had a business in an area that the cartels controlled, they would charge you. But I didn't know that the practice had crept all the way down to taxi drivers.

"But let's talk about more beautiful things," Carlos said, suddenly changing the subject. "Is it cold where you're from?" he asked, and just like that, the conversation moved back to polite hospitality.

I realized then that I was isolated in a different sphere in Mexico, sheltered from the violence that touched many people's lives. I could joke about the rocks on the pavement sign because I had never needed to know its real meaning.

When a cartel controls a territory, it becomes, in essence, a shadow state that even those in power—politicians, businessmen, police— must answer to, leaving the cartel with the supremacy to shape the functions of the government to its liking. Thus cartels have become the de facto government across many areas in Mexico. Two entities— the supposed "legitimate" state and the cartel—semi-functioning atop one another leads to a jumbled mess of corruption and brutality. Those who suffer under this type of system are mainly everyday Mexicans like Carlos who are trying to make a living but constantly finding violence and intimidation in their paths, and Central American migrants who become targets of cartel violence as they pass through Mexico.

Roberto was a migrant from Central America whose ability to earn a living was severely impeded by organized crime. Unlike Carlos,

Roberto left his country when faced with the grim choice of working with the cartels. He sat across from me in the shelter on a sweltering November afternoon in 2016, leaning forward and pressing his interlaced fingers into pursed lips. His searing eyes let me know that he was not naive to the world's many injustices, but that was not going to slow him down. He scrolled through pictures of his girlfriend and infant daughter on his flip phone as he began to explain why he had left them behind.

Roberto had grown up in San Salvador, the capital of El Salvador, which is plagued by gang violence. In a country where only 25 percent of the population completes high school, he was lucky enough to earn a bachelor's degree in computer science. Even with a degree, Roberto emphasized how difficult it was for him to find a job. He worked as a high school computer science teacher for a while, until the school cut his position. One day he attended a government-sponsored job fair, only to find a line of unemployed *salvadoreños* extending out the door. With unlimited options, employers usually hire those they already know, Roberto noted. Without a network of connections, employment in his field seemed unlikely.

Roberto did have a Plan B, which was to open a sandwich shop. The business sustained him temporarily, but like in Mexico, networks of organized gangs surreptitiously control El Salvador. "In some parts of the capital, people hire bodyguards to protect them, so those who really suffer are the poor," Roberto remarked. Because he had a business, the gangs required him to pay "rent," a $500 monthly fee. He paid the quota for a time, but eventually the business just didn't bring in enough money. The gangs then offered him a choice that wasn't really a choice at all: he could do certain "favors" for them, or they would kill him. Roberto knew that if agreed to work for the gangs, it would just be the beginning of an endless cycle of extortion and violence. He thought of his eight-month-old daughter, and couldn't bear to entangle himself in that kind of life. "If your studies no longer serve you and a gang is your only option, what do you do?" Roberto dug his eyes into mine and drew out the silence to the point of awkwardness. "You look for a border."

The ability of the cartels to exert control over state functions extends beyond extorting individual businesses, as in the case of Roberto. The most serious degradation of legitimate statehood comes from the cartels' capacity to keep police and politicians in their back pocket. In a 2010 article entitled "What Do You Want From Us?" the newspaper *El Diario de Juárez* addressed the cartels directly:

> You are at this time the de facto authorities in this city because the legal authorities have not been able to stop our colleagues from falling, despite the fact that we've repeatedly demanded it from them . . . Even war has rules . . . This is why we reiterate, gentlemen of the various narco-trafficking organizations, that you explain what it is you want from us so we don't have to pay tribute with the lives of our colleagues."[9]

Such a plea illustrates how far from legitimate power police and politicians have fallen in Mexico and Central America. Citizens and the media, desperate to stop the violence, have no choice but to appeal to the cartel authorities directly.

In some areas, the police are so thoroughly under the thumb of the cartels that local authorities will block off streets where hit men are planning to carry out assassinations, so that the criminals can escape without notice. Government interrogations of cartel members have also confirmed that many cartel employees will offer a "secret ID code" to police if they are stopped in order to avoid arrest.[10]

Miguel Ortiz was one high-profile example of an officer entangled with a cartel. Ortiz, who helped run La Familia Michoacana until he was arrested in 2010, was also a state police officer for much of his *narco* career. As such, he was able to arrest La Familia's targets (business owners who didn't pay their "rent," journalists, etc.) and then turn them over to the cartel for assassination. Even after he left the force, he still tapped police resources to support La Familia's operations. For instance, in 2009, when the cartel attacked federal police bases in Morelia, Ortiz brought in as many state police vehicles as he could gather. When one of the cartel vans got a flat tire, Ortiz transferred the occupants to police cars, facilitating their escape.[11]

Once a cartel has the local police under their control, they can extend their influence into the political realm by bribing, threatening or assassinating politicians. Rodolfo Torre Cantú was the PRI candidate for governor of Tamaulipas in 2010, and focused his campaign primarily around tougher security measures. Torre Cantú was predicted to win by all the polls, but just a week before the election, gunman open fired on his campaign office, killing him and four of his employees.[12] Although striking and tragic, such assassinations are not uncommon. Even as candidates, politicians have to be mindful about how much to push back against the cartels. When politicians suspect that their lives are in danger, it is easy for the cartels to keep them under control.

When cartels control industry, the police, and politicians, the last piece of the puzzle is the media. Using the press to manipulate the public, many cartels actually *seek* publicity for the crimes they commit, in order to demonstrate to the populace that they're a force to be feared. As Noe Fuentes, a Juaréz criminal, confessed in his interrogation video, "A lot of the attacks are made an hour before news bulletins so they get out to the public."[13] Not only does this tactic spread fear throughout the community, it also lets young gang members know which cartel runs the show—a backward sort of recruitment strategy. Journalists, therefore, are frequently put in the difficult position of either showcasing cartel violence, or censoring news that directly affects the public.

Journalists who don't comply with the cartels often find their lives cut short. Mexico is one of the deadliest countries for a journalist. According to a *New York Times* investigation, at least 104 journalists were murdered in the country between 2000 and 2016, while another twenty-five disappeared and are assumed dead.[14] The Committee to Protect Journalist has recorded at least an additional fourteen journalists murdered between 2017 and 2019.[15] This high death count is not solely caused by cartels; corrupt officials and politicians also surreptitiously order journalists murdered. Nevertheless, the threat to journalists—and by extension, free speech—has created an environment where no one can fully believe the information that is put forth by the news media, which of course benefits the cartels.

During my time in Celaya, I witnessed firsthand how the cartels stretch their malevolent influence into the media. A journalist friend of mine had been reporting on crime for the local paper when she was approached by a group of men who offered to pay her if she refrained from writing about certain topics and highlighted others. Though they did not directly threaten her, she knew that if she refused their offer, her life could be in danger. Accepting the payment, however, would have ensnared her in the cartel's web. The dilemma was not dissimilar to the situation Roberto faced with his sandwich shop. Unlike Roberto, however, my journalist friend had other options for supporting herself. She quit her job at the newspaper and eventually found a job teaching communications.

In addition to the fear of violence and extortion, one of the other serious effects of organized crime's control over the government is a loss of faith in the political and legal system. Citizens begin to feel as if elections don't matter. They worry that if their children are kidnapped, corrupt police officers will not go out of their way to help find them. They become paranoid that anyone—neighbors, coworkers, friends— could be working with the cartel. They also hear stories about ordinary people, the taco man, or the schoolteacher, being hit by stray AK-47 bullets, since cartel assassins often spray obscene amounts of bullets to ensure that they hit their target. As a result, they begin to live in fear of everyone and everything. And if, for whatever reason, the cartel takes an interest in them, their options are either to cooperate, or flee the country.

To be clear, not all parts of Mexico are riddled with *narco* violence and the drug trade does not directly affect every citizen. However, those living in regions where the cartels are in control find their lives being shaped by shadowy figures they may never see or meet, but always fear.

In much of Central America, the violence, extortion, kidnapping, and fear that comes with organized crime is even worse. Honduras and El Salvador tend to compete annually for the highest murder rates in the world. Such violence led to a wave of unaccompanied minors emigrating from Central America starting in 2013, when US Border Patrol detained approximately 80,000 unaccompanied minors in under a year.[16] Since then, an unprecedented number of Central American children and families have come to the US, as gangs have increasingly destabilized the region. In the first five months of fiscal year 2019 (which began in October 2018) alone, the Border Patrol detained 136,150 families with children, up from 107,212 in all of fiscal year 2018.[17] This endemic migration is emblematic of the widespread structures of violence throughout much of Central America.

In Honduras, El Salvador, Guatemala, and parts of Nicaragua, much of this violence comes from the networks of gangs that sprawl across cities and towns, mirroring the gruesome practices of the Mexican cartels. Extortion of businesses is also rampant in these countries. The Honduran newspaper *La Prensa* asserts that in an average year, Salvadorans pay approximately $390 million to gangs, while Hondurans and Guatemalans pay $200 million and $61 million respectively.[18] The ability to extract such sums from business owners highlights just how much power these gangs hold.

As if the devastating gang violence wasn't enough, several of the largest Mexican cartels have begun to expand internationally into many Central American countries. In Guatemala, for instance, the Zetas have taken hold of several territories, extending their drug routes and setting up regional operations. Along with trafficking, the group has carried out massacres as brutal as in Mexico. In 2010, the Guatemalan government declared martial law and fought back, seizing a Zeta training camp. As in Mexico, however, such strikes have simply led the Zetas to launch additional attacks on soldiers and civilians, exacerbating the existing bloodshed.

Similar expansion has occurred in Honduras, as the Sinaloa cartel continues to increase its reach there. Sinaloa (and other cartels) have formed alliances with Honduras' notorious gangs Mara Salvatrucha and Barrio 18. Police believe that several of the killings conducted by these gangs in past years have been ordered by Mexican capos. As one

Honduran official explained, "The Maras are violent anyway—they are a real social problem. But when they get big international organizations behind them like the Mexicans, they are much more threatening. That is the danger we face in the future: the criminals are getting more organized, better armed, and really becoming a problem."[19]

For many Central American migrants that I spoke to in Celaya, the gangs were more than a problem—they were a direct threat to their lives and the lives of their family members. And Central American migrants who do flee their country can't simply leave the violence behind, since as soon as they cross the border into Mexico, they encounter the country's disturbing cartel apparatus. And when the power of cartels has already commandeered politicians, the media, and police units, targeting migrants becomes a tragically easy side business.

Three

"MIS NIÑOS COMEN Y VISTEN"

IN THE REGIONS OF MEXICO where cartel and gang violence are not an ever-present danger, economics tend to be the biggest factor that pushes people north. *"Mis niños comen y visten." My kids eat, they need clothes,* was a line I heard word for word from so many migrants that it felt rehearsed. Only I knew that the sentiment was very real. In Mexico, the minimum wage is 102.68 pesos (approximately $5.45 USD) a day. In Honduras, El Salvador, and Guatemala, minimum wages vary depending on the industry, with the lowest at 214.69 lempiras per day (about $8.76 USD) in Honduras, 3.29 colones a day (about $0.37 USD) in El Salvador, and 82.46 quetzals (approximately $10.77 USD) per day in Guatemala.[1] However, with weak enforcement mechanisms, workers with little to no education are typically paid far below the minimum wage in these places.

Is it possible for a Mexican worker to sustain his family on just over 100 pesos a day? A kilo of tortillas costs around thirteen pesos. A kilo of black beans costs twenty-three. In Celaya, it's hard to find an apartment for less than 2,000 pesos a month. But what about sending your kids to school? Public education is free in theory in Mexico, but everyone has to buy school uniforms, which cost between 200 and 250 pesos, (an expense that often prevents the poorest families from accessing education). It all

Shoppers roam Celaya's downtown market.

adds up, especially when you are earning so little. By comparison, when you can go to the US and make in an hour what would take you days to earn in Mexico, the risks of migrating are pushed aside by the allure of financial stability.

Many migration scholars have also documented the link between increased economic-based migration from Mexico and neoliberal economic policies. The 1994 North American Free Trade Agreement (NAFTA) between Canada, the US, and Mexico significantly reduced the trade barriers between these countries. While the agreement may have benefited some sectors of Mexico's population, those who suffered from NAFTA were mainly the poor and working classes. For instance, in much of southern Mexico, many Indigenous communities traditionally relied on farming to earn a living, selling their goods to local markets. After NAFTA lowered agricultural tariffs and quotas, the markets that once relied on local food were suddenly flooded with inexpensive American products that Indigenous farmers could not compete with. These communities suffered economically, with many people not even able to afford the "cheap" American goods that were theoretically supposed to improve their living standards.[2] As a result, hundreds of thousands of farmers turned to migration as the only viable means of supporting their families.

In northern Mexico, NAFTA also adversely affected many Mexican workers, especially along the border. The agreement made it easier for US companies to move their operations to Mexico for inexpensive labor; many of these companies set up *maquiladoras* (factories) along the US–Mexico border. Because unemployment was so rampant in the areas near the new *maquiladoras,* workers became essentially disposable, allowing factories to pay horrendous wages and subject their workers to long hours and harsh conditions. Additionally, because of the promise of jobs, workers began to flock to border cities such as Juárez and Nogales. As these cities became more and more overcrowded, jobs once again became scarce. When workers were unable to find jobs in the *maquiladoras* or became dissatisfied with the working conditions, crossing the border became a more compelling option.[3]

Trying to Make It Work in Celaya

"Do you have a backpack?" I read his text message while I was waiting in the bustling main square of Celaya. The square was teeming with people—old ladies clustered on the black-painted benches, professionals in transit, teenage couples kissing under the broccoli-shaped hedges. I couldn't spot this friend of a my former student I was going to interview, but he was able to find me because of my flowery and rather childlike backpack.

The interview was awkward from the start. "Hola, Owan," I greeted him, leaning in for the customary half-kiss on the cheek. "It's Jesús," he corrected. I gurgled some unintelligible response as I recalled that first names on Facebook are often different from real ones. We found a spot on one of the densely populated benches in the shade.

Things didn't get any less awkward. When I asked a question, Jesús would often repeat the last part back, pursing his lips while he lightly drummed his chin with two fingers. He was nineteen (but emphasized "I turn twenty this year") and was in many ways a typical young adult overwhelmed by the imminent challenges of work and responsibility. Yet there was something more, a sadness that suggested that life had already defeated him. He had studied human resources at the university where I taught, yet he detested the topic and had been ambivalent about the school and eventually dropped out. He was currently helping his father sell fruit at a stand downtown. His future seemed to be an amorphous ball of unreachable possibility. He enjoyed making YouTube videos and had once even made a video for Celaya's local history museum, but he seemed lost about how to pursue that interest as a career. At bottom, he seemed unexcited about everything.

Since his Celaya routine sparked no passion or sense of opportunity, Jesús held some vision of moving to Chicago. "My whole family is there," he mentioned, referring to his aunts, uncles, cousins, and thirty-one-year-old sister. He painted the image of a life where he could go back to school and eventually make videos professionally, only to subsequently downplay all that with a "well, I don't know." Indeed, he didn't know if this future was possible at all, especially with Donald Trump as president. "Yeah, Trump's way of thinking worries me a little," Jesús offered tentatively, adding, "if someone wants to get permission to live and work there, the (government) doesn't want to grant it anymore."

"Well, at least you get to visit," I offered, although I knew this was no consolation. Since he was eleven, Jesús and his parents had gone every summer to stay with their family in Chicago on a tourist visa.

"We just get the tickets and we go," Jesús noted, in stark contrast to those who spend months aboard a freight train to get to their destination. Despite the difficulties of not speaking much English and adjusting to cultural differences, Jesús fondly recalled the summers he spent in Illinois. However, once he returned to Mexico, he found it difficult to be so far away from his sister. Skype and phone calls helped, but they weren't the same. Jesús had only been nine when she left Mexico, and when he went to visit her in Chicago for the first time two years later, "I almost didn't remember her face when I saw her . . . Yeah, it's been kind of hard."

After a few more one-word answers mixed in with awkward

A flower vendor arranges his stand in Celaya's mercado, where Jesús and his dad also worked.

silences, I asked Jesús if there was anything more he wanted to add about his experiences in the US. He shifted his weight back and forth on the bench as he thought, and I took note of his matching camouflage hat and shorts. "Well I'm not sure this is that important," he said. He then proceeded to tell a story about how one time in Chicago, his cousin gave him a pair of Heely shoes, which he put on, only to fall and break his wrist. While I nodded and laughed at the appropriate places, the story went nowhere. I was searching for something from him, some kind of optimism, or at least an interesting anecdote. But then I realized how difficult it must be for Jesús to summon interest when the world around him seemed like a dead end.

I thought about what it took to sustain oneself in Celaya. A friend of mine taught at three different universities. My former landlord taught full-time at a university, and managed three different properties to stay afloat. My roommate worked eleven-hour days, six days a week, and still confessed that he was struggling financially. And these were people who had advanced degrees and generally good jobs. What about someone like Jesús?

Over the course of the interview, we were interrupted several times by vendors selling all kinds of wares—chocolates and ice cream, purses and backscratchers, unidentifiable vitamins and prayer cards. I remembered walking home from work one day through this very square, trying to avoid the swarm of vendors when I heard someone say my name. I was used to hearing *"güerita"* shouted at me by strangers, but I had never heard my actual name before. I turned to discover two of my students sitting on a bench. They were there working for a photo studio, trying to get parents to purchase baby pictures. They would sit on a bench, wait for a passerby with a baby, and then pitch their professional photos for a very decent price. Long hours, slow work. "And some people are just so rude," one of my students asserted. I immediately felt embarrassed by the times I had been one of those annoyed people bustling past the vendors. This kind of behavior certainly didn't make it any easier for my students, who were just trying to support themselves as they worked their way through college.

As I ended my interview with Jesús, I wondered what I would do in his situation. In Celaya, he could always continue as a vendor, but higher paying jobs were exceedingly rare and demanded substantial

A vendor known as "*El Señor de los Gatitos*" roams the square selling his cat trinkets.

education, which he did not have. So perhaps the deflated, flat tone of the interview was to be expected. After all, neither of us knew what to make of his options for the future.

Yo Soy Trabajador

Determination tucked into the creases in his forehead, Leonardo sat with me in the migrant shelter in Celaya, offering a meticulous description of the first time he had journeyed to the US, just five months before. He diligently named each stop along the way. "From Tierra Blanca I went to Orizaba just on the train. And then from Orizaba I went to La

Lechería . . ." As he mentioned a place, he would tap the table in front of us, as if he was plotting out his journey on an imaginary map. The trip had ended with a deportation from Denver back to his home country of Guatemala. Before being sent back, he had spent a month at a detention center. He described the center as a place where "they feed you pet food. And they intimidate you. There were some people that would cry."

Yet after just five months back in his rural village in Guatemala, Leonardo was back on the road. "It's because of work," he began. "Sometimes there are days when I have work and days when I don't. It's desperation. It's desperation for me because I have always liked to work." For Leonardo, heading north was about having enough to feed and support himself and his family, but it was also about something more. He liked to work. He needed to work. "If a day goes by without work, I get bored and I feel restless," he confessed. As if to bolster this point, he began to emphasize all the things he could do. "I sometimes cut wood. I'm a dockworker too. I'm a dockworker that ships sugar, or really any cargo. And it all raises my morale, but unfortunately there's a lack of jobs. One gets disillusioned when there's no work." I thought about the many days when I felt directionless as a teacher. Still, I had a job. And when my time was up in Mexico, I would head north easily and legally for job prospects in the US.

Job prospects also sent Leonardo north, though he had no family in the US (his mother and fourteen-year-old sister were back in his village in Guatemala). He had chosen New York as his destination. "I'm a dockworker," he repeated once again, when I asked why New York. "I hope to go to New York so that I can find a little job that more or less corresponds to me and I'm going to give it all my effort." While this was the second time he had left his family in less than a year, Leonardo maintained that it was not that difficult to leave because he knew it was a decision he had to make. He told his sister to behave well toward their mother, and set off.

Leonardo had been lucky thus far in avoiding the extortion and assault that the journey north often entailed. Instead of relying on the freight train, he had walked most of the way, in order to avoid the immigration patrol that tended to roam the tracks. He unwrapped his bandaged feet for me, revealing globular callouses and blisters. The one run-in he did have with *la migra* was mostly a conversation. They had stopped him on one of the few times he had tried to board the train. "I'm suffering from hunger," Leonardo told the agents. One of them responded, "Because you want to be, bastard. No one made you leave your house. You did this to yourself." Leonardo then abandoned the idea of taking the train and continued walking.

Reflecting on that encounter in the dim lighting of the shelter, Leonardo told me that he didn't choose to head north. "I did it out of necessity. And because of a lack of work. If there was work, why the hell would we all come here walking?" A surge of frustration animated his voice, yet his neck retreated into the bowl of his shoulders like a turtle simultaneously striking and retreating. "If our country was good, why the fuck would we come here?" Breath slowly seeped out of his clenched mouth, and his tone turned defeated. "Because yes, our country is pretty fucked."

His eyes fixed on the ground between us. A little metal airplane hung from a belt loop on his jeans. I didn't ask him what it meant, but I imagined it had something to do with the future he envisioned for himself. A future where he could take flight from the angst and restlessness and finally find work.

Politics at the Heart of It All

It was a "cold" (sixty-five degrees) December day in Celaya, and we had gathered for the faculty lunch, which was really a gossip session about what was going on at the university. We circled around tortillas, beans, and Coca-Cola in a small classroom, a modular construction with cubicle white walls and random refuse ornamenting the tattered tables. Despite its dismal state, this was one of the few school buildings left that still had walls. Only a few days prior, I had arrived at my classroom prepared to teach, only to find a construction crew literally taking the building apart. Not a student in sight. Why? The county fair, of course. This momentous occasion called for a two-week acceleration in the school closing for the semester in order to set up the event. Education took a backseat to cows, rodeos, and popcorn. The entire faculty found the early closing preposterous, but they accepted it with an "*así es.*"

In the classroom that still had enough walls to mute our voices from administrative ears, the professors began to tell me that they still had no idea whether they would be rehired for the next semester; rumors were circulating that the administration planned on firing the majority of instructors. Everyone was on edge.

"Don't they have to give you enough notice before your contract ends?" I asked as I accepted another glass of soda.

An engineering professor placed his hand on my shoulder and leaned in as if to whisper a secret. He tended to do this when he was explaining something to me, a gesture I interpreted as midway between paternalistic and reassuring. "Kelsey, here's what happens: according to the law, they have to tell us fifteen days before the contract ends. But technically, our contracts don't end until December 31. They're dragging it out to the very end."

This seemed absurd to me, especially given the fact that classes had ended on December 2, yet teachers were required to continue full-time until December 21. While we were supposed to plan our classes for next semester during this time, since no one knew what classes they would be teaching (or if they would even be teaching at all), the days were instead filled with YouTube videos and Facebook. It felt like teacher detention.

Soon the floodgates opened to a litany of complaints about the university's administrators. They were corrupt. They didn't care about the students. They promoted people based on politics, sucking up, and their religion, not because of skills and hard work. As we dug further into the corners of gossip, the university seemed more and more to be an entangled mess of people trying to serve themselves, not the students.

My analytical side wanted to get to the bottom of this. Where were the safeguards against corruption? And then a wider truth emerged: in a country where unemployment is rampant and more education does not necessarily mean a better job, you step on whatever toes you need to in order to get ahead.

My professor friend rested his hand back on my shoulder and responded to my thoughts on the administration's disregard for the students' needs. "The administrators aren't administrators because they care about serving the students. They're in power because they fought for the job security their position holds—because they don't want to be sitting with us in this classroom, wondering if we'll even have a job tomorrow."

These words reminded me of something Leonardo had said at the end of our conversation: "In the US, you can survive." The concept of survival stuck in my mind as I reflected on Leonardo and Jesús, and the thousands of other migrants who had picked up to head north. Survival was what compelled them forward, to make enough to feed their families, or simply to find a job for the sake of their emotional well-being.

PART TWO

THE PRIVILEGE TO CROSS THE BORDER LEGALLY

Four

RACE, CLASS, AND NATIONALITY MATTER

"WHAT DO YOU MEAN THE picture isn't the right size? It's the exact same size as your example." I was stuck, for the second straight day, trying to get my temporary residence visa.

I examined the pictures I had brought in for my file. Right size. White background. Hair pulled back. No jewelry. Not smiling. Check, check, check. I had read the requirements and carefully followed them, yet the immigration officer was ready to send me away.

"No, no. Your face isn't the right size. The picture's taken from too far back. And the background isn't even white." My face may have been slightly smaller than the example, but did that really matter? And the background was white—I had made sure of that. "No, the light makes it look blue," the officer insisted. I grabbed one of the wallet-sized photos, tilting it back and forth. Sure enough, at the right angle, the hue ranged somewhere between blue and gray. Visa denied.

I made one last plea. "I'm so sorry, sir. I thought I had everything, but I guess I didn't know all the requirements. I just arrived from the US, and I took the bus all the way from Celaya to get here. Yesterday I waited two hours at the immigration office in Querétaro to get my paperwork done, but they immediately turned me down. If I go get new photos now, the office will close, and I'll have to come all the way back tomorrow."

The officer mulled it over, considered my imperfect Spanish, my obvious unfamiliarity with his country, and likely, my whiteness. "I'll tell you what," he offered, "I'll leave a note that says you'll bring the right photos when you come to get your fingerprints taken. And right now, I'll process your paperwork without them."

I left the immigration office a short time later, feeling relieved but vaguely unsettled. Wandering the stucco alleyways of San Miguel de Allende, I reflected on what had happened. Seeing a young white American woman, the officer had let me pass, even with mistakes in my file. It was hard to imagine most migrants in the United States, particularly people of color, being afforded the same latitude. On the American side of the border, we tend not to see immigrants as new arrivals, trying to unravel confusing customs, often in an unfamiliar language. Instead, there's an underlying expectation that immigrants should know it all already—how to speak fluid English; how the school system, government and immigration process work; even the nuances of American pop culture.

It was this clear case of privilege in action that left me feeling uncomfortable as I paid the 200 pesos for the bus ride home, and settled into my temporary residence in Celaya.

While my race undeniably expedited my way through Mexico's immigration system, most seeking entry into the United States face the opposite situation. On its most basic level, race, class, and nationality are infused within the fundamental structures of the American immigration system. The more I understood the limited avenues for legal migration, the more it became apparent that US policies are stacked against working-class migrants of color. (This dynamic has only intensified under the Trump presidency.) Access to legal immigration requires a certain degree of privilege that most Mexican and Central American migrants do not possess.

Currently, there are only four avenues to enter the US legally. First, a direct family member with permanent legal status can sponsor a migrant for a visa. However, as highlighted later in this chapter, because of horrendous backlogs in these types of visas, most Mexican and Central American applicants will not be able to get into the US this way.

A second option for legal access is to apply for political asylum when fleeing persecution. In theory, these individuals can turn themselves in at the border and apply for asylum on the grounds that a return to their home country would endanger their lives. In practice, however, receiving asylum is unlikely for most Central Americans and Mexicans. Such a situation also does not exactly connote privilege, since the applicant has to have survived some sort of violence for the asylum request to even be considered.

Third, if one already has a job in the US, their employer can sponsor them via a work visa. Unfortunately, such sponsorships usually only occur for highly skilled workers who have an advanced degree. Currently, 47 percent of Central American[1] and 55 percent of Mexican migrants[2] lack a high school diploma, much less an advanced degree. While a seasonal work visa for immigrant farm workers is theoretically available (an H-2A agricultural visa), most American employers forgo this option, instead relying on undocumented laborers. In fact, H-2A workers only fill an estimated 7 percent of US farm jobs,[3] despite the fact that 33 percent of US agricultural workers are immigrants.[4]

Why do agricultural employers skip this legal option when it is readily available to them? Simply put, it is expensive and cumbersome. Employers spend about $1,000 per H-2A worker for their visa, consulate fees, and transportation to the US, not to mention subsequent housing costs, in addition to the higher wages that an employer typically pays a legal farmworker compared to undocumented laborers. Moreover, employers must go through the laborious process of assuring that no American citizen wants the job before they can sponsor a foreign worker. Since many employers are unwilling or unable to pay these higher costs, very few Mexican and Central American farmworkers are able to get into the United States on an H-2A visa.

The last main option for legal entry is the diversity visa lottery—an annual allotment of 50,000 permanent residence cards distributed randomly to applicants from countries with historically lower US immigration rates. Although President Trump has repeatedly threatened to cut the program, as of 2019, it still remained in effect. Because the visa lottery is intended to encourage diversity in immigrants, Salvadorian and Mexican migrants, among others, are prohibited from applying.[5] Even for the eligible Honduran and Guatemalan migrants, the odds of receiving a green card are very slim. More than 20 million people apply each year; in turn, each applicant has about a .002 percent chance of receiving a greed card.[6] It is literally like winning the lottery.

Given their limited avenues for immigration, it is not surprising that many Central Americans and Mexicans lose faith in finding a legal path across the border. And it is disproportionately poor migrants of color from specific countries who find themselves without legal options, as race, class and nationality all play a fundamental role in determining who is allowed into the United States legally. Dating back over a century, immigration laws have been explicit tools for excluding many poor people from developing countries from legal entry. The Chinese

Exclusion Act, for instance, halted Chinese immigration in 1882 and barred Chinese immigrants from becoming citizens. The law eventually led to national quotas in the 1920s, culminating in the National Origins Act of 1929, which virtually prohibited all Asian immigration and severely restricted immigration from southern and eastern Europe. While immigration law no longer expressly bars people based on their nationality, the current system still hinders lower-class immigrants from developing countries.

Immigration policy often serves as a mirror of our domestic situation, reflecting what the country perceives as an "American" identity. Depending on the current domestic conception of identity, immigration policy fluctuates between stages of nativism and more fluid borders. Modern immigration policy—even before Trump—has largely favored highly skilled workers or those with family legally in the country. While this is an understandable choice, the irony is that this system hurts those with the greatest need—poor, working-class immigrants from impoverished nations.

Although nationality quotas have been phased out, legal scholar Kevin Johnson has highlighted two aspects of current visa law that encumber certain nationalities: country caps and the backlog in visa processing.[7] Instead of barring certain nationalities outright, today's laws prohibit any country from receiving more than 7 percent of the available visas in any one particular category in a given year. This creates a cap on the number of visas a country can receive, which for nations like Mexico, falls well below the number of people who apply. A 2018 State Department report claimed that, "[t]his limit serves to avoid the potential monopolization of virtually all the annual limitation by applicants from only a few countries."[8] While this seems equitable on the surface, it does not take into account the demand for visas.

In Mexico, for example, there was a waiting list of 1,229,505 family and employment sponsorship visas in 2018, for just 25,620 spots. To put that in perspective, the number of people waiting for these visas *worldwide* was 3,791,973. Mexico's visa applicants made up over 30 percent of the total.[9]

This uniformly applied allotment of visas means that if you are an immigrant from Denmark, Sweden, or another country with relatively low immigration rates, you will likely have your visa processed relatively quickly. Mexicans, on the other hand, often have to wait years or even decades before their visas are even considered. For example, in March 2019, the State Department was processing *high priority* visa requests for children of US citizens that had been filed in October 2011. However, the visas for Mexican applicants were so backlogged that the State Department was still processing requests that had been filed in August 1997.[10] These Mexican visa applicants were therefore waiting *twenty-two years* to be able to live in the same country as their parents, and had to wait a full *fourteen years longer* than people from many other countries. Additionally, those waiting for these absurd periods of time are typically the more fortunate migrants because they at least have a resident family member or an employer to sponsor them. For those without family members or high-level skills, there is virtually no way to get into the US legally.

The nations that tend to send large numbers of migrants (and thus have long wait times) are disproportionately countries with higher levels of poverty. Aside from Mexico, the countries with the most applicants on the waiting list for family and employment visas in 2018 were the Philippines (314,229 applicants), India (298,571 applicants), Vietnam (231,519 applicants), China (231,519 applicants), Bangladesh (169,231 applicants), the Dominican Republic

(146,160 applicants), Pakistan (115,625 applicants), Haiti (94,506 applicants), El Salvador (64,868 applicants), and Cuba (55,847 applicants).[11] Not surprisingly, the economic conditions in all these countries tend to be difficult.

Less discussed, however, is that these countries are predominantly non-white. Race therefore matters greatly in the immigration process, as brown and black migrants come from countries with higher immigration rates and thus face prohibitively long wait times that effectively block any legal path for them to get into the US. Though racial quotas barring certain immigrants no longer drives immigration law (with the strikingly racist exception of President Trump's four attempted bans on immigrants from several majority-Muslim countries), this legacy of discrimination has had a lasting effect on modern American immigration policy.[12]

Laws regarding citizenship have long been used to draw dividing lines between those who "belong" in the United States, and those who are considered outsiders. Of course, for much of American history, those who belonged were exclusively white people. The Naturalization Act of 1790, for example, limited citizenship solely to "free white persons." Subsequent immigration law was designed to treat non-white people as largely ineligible for citizenship. The purpose of the 1910 national origin quota was explicitly to "confine immigration as much as possible to western and northern European stock."[13] Such ideas culminated in the implementation of the National Origin Quota in 1924, which set an annual quota of 150,000, and limited each nationality to 2 percent of the number of its countrymen already in the United States. This quota system institutionalized the national perception that certain races of immigrants were more desirable than others.

The notion that Latino (particularly Mexican) immigrants were less desirable than other groups can be traced back to the "repatriation campaign" of the 1930s. Sparked by the economic strife of the Great Depression and the growing concern regarding a supposed deluge of Mexican immigrants, the government rounded up almost a half-million Mexican-Americans, *many of whom were US citizens,* and deported them to Mexico.[14] Notably, during the same time, the US allowed over 700,000 new immigrants to enter the country. Many of these new arrivals were European refugees, and their admission was granted without regard to the previous quotas.[15] Thus, while the government was deporting Mexican residents and citizens, it was simultaneously making a legal exception for European noncitizens. The repatriation campaign marked a fundamental shift that painted Mexican and Latin American immigrants as a threat to the political and economic stability of the country.

A decade after the repatriation campaign, President Franklin Delano Roosevelt signed an executive order that established the nation's largest guest worker system, known as the Bracero Program. Due to concerns that World War II would create agricultural labor shortages, Mexico and the US agreed to allow over 4.6 million contracts specifically for Mexican farmworkers to come to the US on a temporary basis.[16] The program, however, was incredibly controversial, since agricultural employers ignored many of the rules in place to protect Mexican workers, and widespread human rights abuses were reported.

Just as the Bracero Program was being shut down in the 1960s, President John F. Kennedy repealed the National Origin Quotas.[17] Although many regarded this decision as the end of race-based immigration law, the barriers that disadvantaged immigrants of certain races by no means disappeared. While removing the national origin quotas, the law implemented the worldwide quota restriction previously mentioned. These restrictions had a negative effect on Mexicans, as the visa cap placed on Mexican immigration was far below the number of workers who had been permitted to enter the country through the Bracero Program. Because the demand for cheap agricultural labor didn't cease, the lack of legal ways to work in the US created a market for undocumented labor. The incredibly long wait for legal entry, paired with the market for undocumented labor, caused illegal immigration to rise steadily over the next several decades.

The 7 Percent Non-Solution

People of color have been disenfranchised over the course of American history in myriad ways, and immigration policy is no exception. The requirement that migrants have either a legal family member or an employer who can sponsor them in order to be eligible for a visa severely curtails their ability to enter the US legally. Because people of color have historically been restricted or excluded from migrating via national origin quotas, current migrants of color are less likely to have a legal resident family member to sponsor their entry. As previously mentioned, without this link to a legal family member, employer, or a special skill, there is literally no way to get into the country legally.

The second main historical legacy that still perpetuates a system of racial exclusion is the uniformly applied national quotas. When Mexico and Norway both have access to a maximum of 7 percent of annual visas in each category, it disproportionately strains the system for Mexican immigrants. Not only does this disenfranchise immigrants based on their nationality, but it also unevenly affects people of color, since colonizing (developed) and whiter countries tend to send less migrants to the US and thus experience much less of a visa backlog. This is evidenced by the fact that none of the previously mentioned countries with the highest number of migrants waiting for family and employment visas are predominantly white.[18] Because they have very few options for legal entry, undocumented workers in America are much more likely to be people of color from low economic classes.

The Trump administration has further exacerbated racial exclusion in immigration policy by scrapping several legal avenues that principally apply to people of color. These actions, while devastating, are not surprising, given how Trump has belittled nonwhite immigrants. Examples of his racist rhetoric abound. Trump has claimed, among other things, that Haitian immigrants "all have AIDS," and that Nigerians would never "go back to their huts" after coming to America.[19] He has relentlessly depicted Muslim immigrants as terrorists[20] and portrayed Central American and Mexican immigrants as invaders, rapists, and subhuman.[21] He has also notoriously disparaged immigrants from "shithole countries," meaning those from El Salvador, Haiti, and several African nations.[22] While he rails against immigrants of color, Trump simultaneously asks why the US can't have more people from countries like Norway.[23] The racist backdrop of the president's immigration strategy is unmistakable.

Such rhetoric has led to numerous policies that further narrow legal options for specific people of color. In 2017 and 2018, for instance, Trump tried to retract the Temporary Protected Status (TPS) of Salvadorian, Haitian, Nicaraguan, and Sudanese people, who had been previously allowed entry because of catastrophic natural disasters, armed conflicts, and other specific conditions in their home countries.[24] Had the courts not struck down this decision, it would have removed the legal status from thousands of people of color. Similarly, the Trump administration's attempts to rescind Deferred Action for Childhood Arrivals (DACA), if successful, would remove protections for nearly 700,000 young people, 94 percent of whom are Latino.[25] In perhaps the most emblematic example, just after his inauguration in 2017, Trump barred non-citizens from seven countries (five majority Muslim and all predominantly nonwhite) from admission.[26] This policy, upheld by the Supreme Court, harkens back to the racial exclusion policies of the previous century. In the Trump era, no one can remotely claim that immigration policy is divorced from its racist past.

"Give me your tired and your poor who can stand on their own two feet and who will not become a public charge."

Americans have long been particularly fearful of poor immigrants infiltrating the country, overwhelming social programs and swallowing up public benefits that should, in their view, be reserved for citizens. Such sentiment still proliferates the national discourse in 2019. In one of several examples of this narrative, Ken Cuccinelli, the director of United States Citizenship and Immigration Services under Donald Trump, commented on the Emma Lazarus poem at the base of the Statue of Liberty, changing the words to those in the quote above.[27] He also claimed that the original poem was just referring to people coming from Europe. Just prior to this remark, the Trump White House released a statement saying, "We must ensure that non-citizens do not abuse our public benefit programs and jeopardize the social safety net needed by vulnerable Americans."[28] Such rhetoric operates under the false premise that allowing poor immigrants into the US will jeopardize the benefits available to citizens.

This fundamental idea has led to the creation of specific requirements intended to exclude those who are perceived to be a threat to resources. One such mechanism for doing so is the public charge exclusion, which, under the Immigration and Nationality Act, bars any immigrant who is deemed likely to become a public charge—that is, someone who relies on public assistance—from receiving legal status. While this doctrine has long been a backdrop of immigration law, it has gained increased enforcement mechanisms over time. For example, the 1965 Immigration and Naturalization Act ordered that the State Department consider the age, health, family status, assets, resources, financial status, and education of an applicant before granting a visa.[29]

The problem is that determining who might become a public charge solely based on this information is not a formulaic process, leaving ample room for subjectivity and prejudice. Additionally, this doctrine operates under the faulty assumption that those lacking resources in their home countries will continue to languish economically in the United States. Such a notion blatantly contradicts the ideal that access to the American Dream allows even the poorest of the poor to thrive. In reality, there is no way to gauge if the world's poorest immigrants will prosper in the "land of opportunity" because the public charge exclusion allows the State Department to deny them this chance.

On top of this faulty moral premise, there is also very little oversight and review of decisions made by consular officers (who review visa applications). As legal scholar Richard Boswell remarks, "The ability to grant or deny visas without judicial review places enormous power in the hands of the consular officer."[30] In the last few decades, the government has implemented a system where the Visa Office at the State Department advises on some visa decisions. However, since the consular officer briefs the State Department representative, they generally accept the officer's version of the facts and are unlikely to do significant probing on their own. Other than this advisory system, very few checks and balances exist in the visa review process, which exacerbates the already arbitrary nature of the public charge exclusion.

The public charge exclusion came to the forefront again in 1996, when the Illegal Immigration Reform and Immigrant Responsibility Act raised the qualifications and responsibility for those who sponsored immigrants. The law required sponsors to pledge that they would assume full financial responsibility for the person they sponsored. It also mandated that that the income of the sponsor exceed 125 percent of the federal poverty line. The sponsor's financial responsibility continues until the immigrant has worked at least ten years or has become a naturalized citizen.[31]

While the public charge exclusion applies to both visa applicants and immigrants already in the United States, it historically has been applied most frequently to those soliciting a visa. From 1981 to 1990, the State Department denied approximately 10 percent of all applicants on public charge grounds, while just a dozen people already residing in the US were deported on the same basis. In 1997, the public charge exclusion was the most common grounds for visa denial, with 39,077 applicants denied because of it.[32] Denying poor immigrants legal entry into the US is therefore not just an extreme idea; it has been an actual practice for decades.

Under Donald Trump, the public charge exclusion has gained a new level of ferocity, as the administration has embraced the familiar narrative that immigrations are overwhelming public benefits. On January 2, 2018, the administration published revised portions of the Foreign Affairs Manual (FAM) relating to the public charge exclusion, which shifted how consular officers approached incoming visas. Before these revisions, applicants could summit an affidavit of support from their sponsor in order to overcome factors that might lead them to be deemed a public charge. However, under the adjusted FAM, a sponsor's affidavit of support is no longer sufficient to overcome potential negative flags in an application. Now, the officer can also consider the sponsor's past or current receipt of public benefits when making a decision. Additionally, the amendments to the FAM allow officials to take into account whether any of the applicant's family members received public benefits.[33] These changes in the FAM supplement considerations already applied (age, health, income, education level, and family situation), combining to make it extremely difficult for working-class migrants to gain legal entry into the US.

By March 2019, Trump's changes to the FAM had already affected the number of migrants being denied on public charge grounds. According to a study by the National Foundation for American Policy, the overall number of immigrant visas that were denied by the State Department increased by 39 percent from 2017 to 2018.[34] This increase is due at least in part to the changes to the FAM, which caused the public charge exclusion to be more readily implemented. In 2017, there were 3,237 visas denied on the basis of public charge, versus 13,450 in 2018—a 316 percent increase.[35] This means that in just one year, over 13,000 working-class migrants were not allowed into the US explicitly because of their class.

To even further exacerbate the reprehensible effects of the public charge exclusion, in August 2019, Trump announced an unprecedented expansion of the law. First, the administration changed the definition of a public charge from someone who relies on public benefits for the majority of their income to someone who receives any number of benefits for more than twelve months. This new definition allowed consular officers to consider receipt of aid such as Medicaid, food stamps and housing assistance as grounds for denial under the public charge exclusion. It also permitted English deficiency to be considered a negative factor in one's application. On the other hand, a household income of at least 250 percent of the federal poverty level became a heavily weighted positive factor in the public charge test.[36] Several lawsuits challenged these rules after they were announced, and on October 11, 2019, they were struck down by a federal court. However, if the administration appeals and these rules are ever put into effect, these changes to the already faulty public charge system would multiply the number of poor immigrants denied legal status.

Overall, the public charge exclusion perpetuates the idea that the neediest immigrants will be the least likely to contribute to society. This notion originates from engrained stereotypes regarding poor immigrants'—particularly poor immigrants of color—lack of contribution to society. Such a sentiment is evidenced by Trump's previously mentioned rhetoric toward nonwhite immigrants, which do not stem from any kind of systematic evidence. Such stereotypes have deep consequences: in this case, they work to exclude poor (and nonwhite) immigrants who attempt to "do the right thing" and get through the system legally.

In addition to doctrines such as the public charge exclusion, the limited amount of work visas—particularly for moderately skilled and unskilled personnel—disenfranchises working class immigrants, as the number of visas available is not remotely calibrated to the US demand for labor. This discrepancy creates and sustains a market for undocumented labor. The very few accessible work visas are overwhelming intended for highly skilled workers, which is not surprising given that the government has always made room for those who it deems most likely to contribute to society. However, prioritizing highly skilled workers ignores the fact that many of the country's lowest paying jobs rely on immigrant labor. When jobs exist, but a legal means of entering the country does not, migrants are lured by the promise of economic prosperity, but still face a life with deportation hanging over their heads, compounded by a lack of protections and decent wages in the workplace. This is a reality that white middle-and-upper class migrants from nations with low immigration rates do not face, as they are basically allowed to charge forward through the ducts of the immigration bureaucracy, never having to encounter the monstrous violence of the journey north.

Five

THE COMPLICATIONS OF ASYLUM

BEFORE THERE WERE REPORTS OF officers refusing asylum to migrants at the southern border; before asylum seekers were moved to Mexico to await their hearings; and before Central Americans had to exhaust asylum options in other countries before applying to enter the United States, there was Evelia. We spoke in July 2017 about her attempts to solicit asylum, before this legal right had become the focus of the Trump administration. In May of the previous year, Evelia and her three daughters had taken a bus to Tijuana, then turned themselves in to immigration authorities at the border, seeking asylum. Evelia was fortunate that her cousin, a legal resident living in Oregon, could vouch for her, and thus the family was only detained briefly before they were released to join Evelia's cousin.

Unlike many of my migrant interviews, Evelia and I were not meeting at the shelter in Celaya, but rather at the Latino Community Association in Bend, Oregon. Framed by the white office walls, Evelia's river of black hair was smoothed against her scalp into a ponytail that cascaded down to her hips. Her pink socks were dotted with sheep. She was chatty from the start, imparting a concerto of words so constant that there was little room for my occasional murmurs of agreement. For almost three hours, we browsed through her life story—frequently taking long detours for her to share memories of her daughters.

Evelia and her husband had been raising their girls in Chilapa de Alvarez, Guerrero, a mid-sized city in southwest Mexico. Chilapa is about 200 miles from Iguala, where forty-three students from the *Ayotzinapa* Rural Teachers' College infamously disappeared in 2014, to the horror of the international community. Guerrero is Mexico's most violent state, as a surge in opium production allowed cartels to take control over the local government. In 2016 alone, more than 2,844 people were murdered in Guerrero, often in particularly gruesome ways.[1] "We applied for asylum because there's so much violence in Mexico," Evelia began, her expression poised, her face glowing despite the topic. "Where we were living with my mother, it's so violent. My cousin told me that (coming to the US) was a better future for the girls."

For Evelia and her family, the shift toward extreme violence in Chilapa de Alvarez was stark. "Before, everything was really calm," Evelia said, glancing down at her shoes, the abundant moles on her face scattered like stars across a round horizon. "But then there was a time in which they kidnapped two guys that were students. That was when we started to see more ugliness. They started to kill, to kidnap." By "they," Evelia was referring to the network of gangs and cartels that had infiltrated the state.

When the violence was just beginning to affect everyday citizens, Evelia and her husband left to find work in a nearby larger city. Economic opportunities were scarce in the region, and bigger cities provided more hope for employment. Evelia's daughters stayed behind with their grandmother in Chilapa de Alvarez. However, the violence in the city grew worse. During one phone call, the *abuela* reported that three students at the local middle school had been targeted by cartel violence.

"The middle school is there on the same route that I used to walk with my daughters," Evelia recalled in the Latino Community Association's quiet office. "Two of the boys," she continued, "they burned them with gasoline." She paused, letting the gravity of such an event thicken the room with the musty smell of tragedy. "They burned them," Evelia repeated softly, shaking her head in disbelief. She leaned into the wall and let her head go limp against it. "They say that one escaped. But before they burned them, they read them some messages that said that they were going to grab some of their parents and kill them." It was difficult to know why these particular students had been targeted. Perhaps their parents had aggravated cartel members. Or maybe the cartels were simply trying to send a message of fear to the community. Whatever the reason, Evelia's reaction was same as many other parents: she no longer let her children go outside by themselves.

Shortly after the boys' murder, Evelia's mother reported another morbid episode. "She told us, 'You know what *hija,* in the route that the girls take (to school), I went to drop them off . . . next to the path were two dead people that had been dumped there. We found them there headless, dead on the side of the path.'" I tried to imagine what it must have been like for Evelia's daughters to see the corpses, discarded like pieces of festering trash. To protect her children, Evelia had to restrict the borders of their lives even further. "I told my husband, you know what, the girls aren't going to school anymore . . . It doesn't matter if they miss the rest of the school year. I just want them to be okay." Evelia returned to Chilapa de Alvarez, where she and her daughters spent their days afraid to leave their house. She knew it was time for them to leave Mexico.

Instead of subjecting her family to the dangers of crossing the border illegally, Evelia decided to try for political asylum in the United

States. There are two ways to apply for asylum: either defensively or affirmatively. Defensive applicants are those who are either apprehended at the border or inside the US, while affirmative applicants turn themselves in to immigration authorities before crossing the border (like Evelia). Once they have filled out an application, affirmative applicants are granted an interview with an asylum officer. Based just on that interview, the officer has the power to either grant asylum, deny it, or pass the case on to the regional immigration court. The majority of cases are passed on to the court, which has the sole authority to decide the migrant's fate.

As we will discuss later in this chapter, the Trump administration has sought to systematically dismantle asylum for Central Americans by making the process so cumbersome that most migrants cannot even apply. However, regardless of whether or not these policies stick, for Mexicans and Central Americans, political asylum is still nearly impossible to attain. According to data from the Transactional Records Access Clearinghouse at Syracuse University, Mexican applicants consistently have the highest rate of denials when it comes to asylum cases, closely followed by Haitians, Hondurans, Guatemalans, and Salvadorians. In 2019, Mexicans soliciting asylum were denied 88 percent of the time, while Hondurans, Guatemalans, and Salvadorians were denied in 86 percent, 86 percent, and 82 percent of cases respectively. Meanwhile those most likely to win their cases (Syrians) were denied only 5 percent of the time.[2]

Why is there such a notable difference in denials when the Northern Triangle (which is made up of Guatemala, Honduras, and El Salvador) and many Mexican states are often classified as the most dangerous regions in the world? Because fleeing drug- or gang-related violence often does not fall under the asylum definition of persecution. To qualify as a refugee, a migrant must be unwilling or unable to return to their country due to persecution "on account of race, religion, nationality, membership in a particular social group, or political opinion."[3] Asylum law does not explicitly include victims of drug- and cartel-related violence. Additionally, those applying for asylum must show that their home government will not protect them, forcing them to take refuge in another country. The typical asylum grantee, therefore, tends to be someone fleeing dictators and civil wars, where the persecutor is unmistakably part of the government.

For most people fleeing drug violence in Central America or Mexico, "membership in a particular social group" is the only asylum category that might apply. Some immigration lawyers argue that their clients fit this category based on their familial ties (many gangs will attack a person based on their relation to someone on their hit list). However, successful asylum seekers must also show persecution on behalf of government-linked entities because of their membership in a certain group. Given that the line between cartels/gangs and the government is often fuzzy in Mexico and Central America, proving these linkages is extremely difficult. For example, immigration judges can decide that police officers murdering and torturing for a cartel or gang are rogue officers who are not acting on behalf of the state. Such rulings, however, ignore the ways in which state institutions and organized crime are twisted together, forming an indiscernible braid across much of Mexico and the Northern Triangle.

In addition to the difficulty of proving that migrants fit the strict definition of a refugee, experts suggest that the national discourse in the United States that often frames Central American and Mexican migrants as "gaming the system" may impact decisions in the immigration courts. According to asylum attorneys Eduardo Beckett and Carlos

Spector, who work out of El Paso, Mexican applicants were systematically disenfranchised in this process even in the pre-Trump era. "There is an institutionalized policy of discouraging Mexican applicants by prolonged detention and serious resistance by government attorneys in immigration court," Spector noted back in 2010, before the bigoted discourse of the Trump era took the national stage. In Spector's experience, the government often puts multiple or more experienced lawyers on the case when the defendant is Mexican. "They want to send a message that if you go to the US for asylum, you're going to get fucked. You are going to be detained and then denied."[4]

It is also evident that receiving asylum can be highly dependent on the asylum officer or judge who decides the case. A study done by the *Stanford Law Review* found that immigration judges in the same district who were reviewing applicants from the same country produced highly different decisions. In one region, an asylum officer did not grant asylum to a single Chinese applicant, while two other officers in the same region granted asylum to 68 percent of Chinese applicants. In another area, the mean rate for granting asylum to Chinese applicants was 57 percent at the time of the study. However, four of the officers in the region granted asylum to less than 5 percent of Chinese cases, while twelve other officers granted asylum to more than 90 percent of Chinese applicants.[5]

Why would there be such variability among judges and officers within the same region in processing applicants from the same country? When processing an asylum claim, the officer or judge must consider two factors. First, they must evaluate the evidence to determine whether the applicant's claim fits into the legal definition of refugee, as discussed earlier. Secondly, they must consider whether they believe the applicant is telling the truth. This latter consideration is even more subjective than the first. While there are some facts that an officer or judge might be able to validate with home country consulates or law officials, many of the pieces of an applicant's story simply can't be confirmed. Without proof, it's up to the officer or judge to decide, which leaves ample room for personal opinions. According to a *Reuters* report, judges who are male, are former ICE prosecutors, or who are new to their position are far more likely to order an applicant deported. The same report highlighted the case of two Honduran women, both of whom were targeted by gangs because of their involvement in the same parent-teacher association. Both fled and applied for asylum, but the woman who applied in San Francisco was granted asylum, while her friend who applied in Charlotte, North Carolina was ordered deported.[6] Such an example points to a troubling trend—a judge's background and political opinion may have more of an impact on an asylum case than the facts themselves.

With the current national discourse perpetuating blatant racism against Latino immigrants, and President Trump claiming that Mexicans and Central Americans scam the asylum system so that they can get released into the US, racism surely comes into play in at least some judge's perceptions of asylum seekers. Without a fully objective process, Mexican and Central American immigrants who aim to enter the country legally are placed at an acute disadvantage.

Catch and Detain

There is no question that, under President Trump, attempts to systematically disadvantage Mexican and Central American migrants in the asylum process have become markedly more zealous. After all, this has been the express intent of his administration. In November 2018, Trump tweeted, "Catch and Release is an obsolete term. It is now

Catch and Detain. Illegal Immigrants trying to come into the USA, often proudly flying the flag of their nation as they ask for US Asylum, will be detained or turned away."[7] Trump has insistently pushed the idea that asylum seekers exaggerate their stories and then disappear before their actual hearings take place. At an April 2019 speech before the Republican Jewish Coalition, Trump called the asylum program a "scam," and went on to describe asylum seekers as "[s]ome of the roughest people you've ever seen, people that look like they should be fighting for the UFC." He continued: "They read a little page given by lawyers that are all over the place—you know lawyers, they tell them what to say. You look at this guy, you say, 'wow, that's a tough cookie . . . No, no, he'll do the accosting.'"[8]

This simplistic and demonizing messaging not only mischaracterizes refugees to promote fear and ignores the looming threats they face, but also disregards the evidence that they overwhelmingly comply with the byzantine asylum process. According to Department of Justice data, in fiscal year 2018, 89 percent of all asylum applicants attended their final court hearing to receive a decision on their case. Among those with access to legal representation, this rate jumped to 98 percent.[9] This fact alone completely nullifies the claim that asylum seekers use the legal process as a loophole to get across the border so that can disappear into the country. Regardless, Trump's relentless insistence on this false premise underlies several policy changes to asylum intended to deter Central Americans and Mexicans from even pursuing this right.

Across the board, the Trump administration has sought to severely restrict legal immigration, with narrowing asylum as the starkest example. As early as May 2017, before asylum policies had changed, human rights groups began to report on border patrol agents turning away asylum seekers without granting them the required screening, and coercing them into returning to Mexico.[10] In one of many examples in a Human Rights First report, in February 2017, border patrol agents pressured a Mexican asylum seeker named Magdalena into recanting her fears about returning home. Magdalena had fled the state of Guerrero after cartel members sexually assaulted her and made her watch videos of torture. She applied for asylum three times at the Ped-West port of entry, but each time she was manipulated and then turned away.

On her second asylum attempt, an agent asked Magdalena if she had heard about the new president and explained that he was only offering asylum to Christians. He then asked Magdalena if she was afraid to go with the Mexican immigration officers in Tijuana, to which she replied that she didn't know them and therefore had no idea whether to be afraid. "That is not what I'm asking," the agent reportedly replied. "Are you afraid to go with these officials?" When she replied "no," he responded, "Well then you have to answer 'no' to the question 'are you afraid.'" He then turned on a video recorder to document her answer. When she tried to apply again a few days later, she was told, "You will never get asylum in the United States," and made to return to Mexico.[11] Although such manipulation of the process is explicitly against the law, it highlights how Trump's rhetoric toward asylum seekers—in this case, only a month after his inauguration—has trickled down to the on-the-ground agencies that feel legitimized in their dehumanizing treatment of migrants.

Remain in Mexico

In addition to amped up hostility at the border, legal asylum policies have fundamentally shifted under the Trump administration. This began in June 2018, with a decision by then-Attorney General Jeff Sessions which overturned a case granting asylum to a domestic violence victim. Sessions ruled that, "Claims by aliens pertaining to domestic violence or gang violence perpetrated by nongovernmental actors will not qualify for asylum," thus undermining the very legal argument that many immigration lawyers had relied upon to protect the lives of migrants fleeing gang violence.[12] In doing so, Sessions and the Department of Justice set a precedent that victims of private criminal activity do not constitute a "particular social group" for purposes of an application for asylum.

Although the Sessions ruling was certainly significant, the most alarming changes to asylum law occurred in 2019, beginning with a policy the Trump administration ironically deemed the "Migrant Protection Protocols." When the administration launched the policy (popularly known as "Remain in Mexico") in January 2019, it forced all those who sought asylum along the southern border to return to Mexican border cities while their cases slogged through the immigration courts, a process that often takes years. The policy, intended to deter asylum seekers along the southern border (who are primarily Mexican and Central American), has fundamentally eroded the right to seek refuge. Not only has it caused chaos and confusion as migrants go through the legal process, but it has put those seeking safety at serious risk. As of October 2019, nearly 50,000 migrants had already been returned to Mexico under the policy, including 16,000 asylum applicants under the age of eighteen.[13] If "Remain in Mexico" stays in effect, the number of migrants affected will only continue to rise.

In returning scores of innocent persons seeking asylum to border towns, Trump placed the most vulnerable population in one of the most crime-ridden areas, a flagrant recipe for disaster as well as a blatant disregard of human rights. Many migrants have been returned to Tijuana and Ciudad Juarez, which are consistently among the top five Mexican cities with the highest level of homicides in the country. The homicide rate in Ciudad Juárez has continued to increase, rising to 107 murders per 100,000 people in 2019, paired with a 100 percent increase in kidnappings compared to 2018. Similarly, Tijuana has been named the world's most violent city by Mexico's Citizens' Council for Public Safety and Criminal Justice.[14] Other asylum seekers have been returned to Matamoros, Nuevo Laredo, and Mexicali, similarly violent border cities. This inherent risk is compounded by the fact that those who make these cities dangerous (cartels, gangs, and random criminals) routinely prey on migrants. By August 2019, Human Rights First and other humanitarian groups had already documented 116 cases of migrants being raped, assaulted, kidnapped, or persecuted after returning to Mexico under the "Remain in Mexico" policy.[15] This number is likely a gross underestimate, given the difficulty of documenting such violence.

For those awaiting asylum in border cities, their lives remain volatile and uncertain. Many organizations are trying to help those affected by "Remain in Mexico," yet there is little they can do to protect them from gang and cartel violence. Migrant shelters in border cities are incredibly overcrowded. When every shelter is filled ten times beyond its capacity, security systems become compromised, making it easier for organized crime to infiltrate. Those who are turned away from shelters and find themselves on the streets are even more likely to be targeted.

To avoid this perilous fate, migrants have two (largely ineffective) exemptions to avoid being returned to Mexico. First, they can try to prove that they will face persecution in Mexico on account of their "race, religion, nationality, membership of a particular social group or political opinion."[16] Yet as discussed previously, demonstrating that you will be targeted based on these grounds is exceedingly difficult for victims of gang/cartel violence. The other option is to apply for an exemption under the Convention Against Torture, which holds that a state cannot expel a person to another state "where there are substantial grounds for believing that he would be in danger of being subjected to torture."[17] While fear of torture may apply to many Central American migrants returned to Mexico, illustrating that there are "substantial grounds" for this concern is problematic. Additionally, both of these exemptions stipulate that the migrant must prove that it is "more likely than not" that they will face persecution or torture in order for these protections to apply. This high bar is nearly impossible to attain. In the meantime, those who face substantial risks but cannot definitively prove them have no legal protections.

Even those who might qualify to stay in the US are unlikely to know that they have the right to apply for an exemption, as border agents are not required to ask asylum seekers whether they fear persecution or torture before they are returned. If a migrant does explicitly express these fears, they are interviewed by a US Citizenship and Immigration Services asylum officer to determine if it is "more likely than not" that they will face these dangers if they are sent back. Again, most migrants have no idea that they have the right to receive such an interview. As of June 2019, only 747 people have explicitly expressed a fear of returning to Mexico. Of these 747 people, 629 were still returned because of the nearly impossible standard for proving these fears.[18] By October 2019, less than 1 percent of migrants affected by "Remain in Mexico" had been transferred out of the program.[19]

Third Country Transit Asylum Ban

As if "Remain in Mexico" wasn't enough of an assault on the principles of asylum and fundamental justice, in July 2019 the Trump administration announced the egregious Third Country Transit Asylum

Ban. Under this policy, migrants who pass through another country before coming to the United States must solicit asylum in that country and receive a denial before they can then apply for asylum in the US. The devastating effects of such a policy cannot be overstated. The ban applies to all non-Mexican asylum seekers at the southern border, which are the vast majority of asylum seekers. As such, they are forced to either solicit asylum in Mexico or Guatemala under the absurd premise that these countries can guarantee their safety, or try to cross into the US illegally.

According to the Trump administration, the premise of the ban is that if a migrant doesn't apply for asylum in the first country they enter, they must not be in grave danger. This nonsensical idea assumes that a Guatemalan migrant, for instance, would be just as safe in Mexico as they would in the United States. However, because of the transnational nature of many Central American gangs, these migrants can usually be easily located once they arrive in Mexico, making it impossible for them to fully escape the threats that caused them to flee in the first place. Similarly, Salvadorian or Honduran migrants would likely be no safer in Guatemala than they would be at home, since Guatemala's murder rate is among the highest in the world.[20] Furthermore, as discussed in detail in the following chapters, the rates at which Central American migrants are assaulted, kidnapped, raped, and murdered in Mexico are astounding. Simply put, Central American migrants are not safe in Mexico. To pretend otherwise represents a flagrant distortion of the political realities south of the border.

The Third Country Transit Asylum Ban also assumes that Guatemala and Mexico have asylum systems that would be able to process large amounts of applicants. This is decidedly not the case. Guatemala, for instance, received 259 asylum applications in 2018.

None of these applications were approved, largely because of the lack of institutional infrastructure to review these cases.[21] While Mexico receives and processes more applications, its asylum system is still afflicted by chronic understaffing, backlogs and a fundamental lack of access. The Mexican Commission for Refugee Aid (COMAR), the agency that manages the asylum process, only has four offices around the country. A 2018 report by Amnesty International found that 75 percent of migrants surveyed were never informed of their legal right to asylum, which is required by Mexican law. The report also noted that officials frequently turned back Central American asylum seekers without allowing them to apply.[22] To make matters worse, COMAR's 2019 budget was slashed by 20 percent, making it even more difficult to offer asylum to the thousands of migrants no longer able to apply in the US. Even before this budget cut, COMAR was only able to process 5,700 applicants in 2018.[23] Requiring migrants to seek asylum via systems that lack fundamental access is akin to shutting down their right to seek refuge entirely.

Like "Remain in Mexico," migrants affected by the Third Country Transit Asylum Ban can apply for exemptions, also under the Convention Against Torture or the Immigration and Nationality Act, under the premise that they will be tortured or persecuted in the transit country based on their race, nationality, religion, membership in a particular social group, or political opinion. Once again, migrants have to affirmatively state these specific fears in order for officials to consider that they are "more likely than not" to occur. Migrants who can prove they are victims of severe forms of trafficking can also apply for an exemption to the policy, but this represents a sliver of applicants. Unaccompanied minors are not exempted from the ban. Of course, this policy has faced significant legal challenges, but in September

2019, the Supreme Court ruled that the policy could remain in effect while the legal battle continued.

The Trump administration has sought to justify the asylum ban by repeatedly trying to coerce Mexico, Guatemala and even Panama into signing a Safe Third Country agreement. The United States currently has such an agreement with Canada, which requires asylum seekers to apply in whichever country they enter first, operating under the idea that both nations offer similar protections and have robust asylum systems. Although Mexico and Panama have resisted signing a Safe Third Country agreement, in July 2019, President Jimmy Morales of Guatemala signed such a deal with Trump. The terms of the deal were incredibly unclear, and could potentially allow the government to deport all asylum seekers to Guatemala, even those who never even transited through the country. To be sure, the agreement will face legal challenges, and just after the deal was signed, Guatemala's Constitutional Court ruled that President Morales could not unilaterally sign without the approval of the country's Congress. With a new Guatemalan president taking over in January 2020, the fate of the deal could be in flux. Nevertheless, even pursuing such an absurd agreement is just another example of the Trump administration's attempts to end legal avenues for immigration.

Ultimately, the purpose of "Remain in Mexico," the Third Country Transit Asylum Ban, and the potential agreement with Guatemala is to deter Mexican and Central American migrants from seeking asylum by rendering the legal process so burdensome that it is effectively unavailable. And on top of the legal obstacles, all three policies put migrants at grave risk, taking away their fundamental right to safety—a value that used to be at the heart of asylum law in the United States.

"Gracias a Dios, ahorita estamos bien."

Where do those fleeing for their lives turn when asylum is no long a viable option? For Fernando, a migrant escaping gang violence in Tegucigalpa, Honduras, the answer was to cross illegally. Fernando was deported from the US in May 2016, even before Trump was elected and his administration trashed the asylum system for Central Americans. Five months later, he again attempted to enter the country. After hearing his story, one of the immigration officers that detained him encouraged him to apply for political asylum. The officer assured Fernando that with the looming threats to his life in Honduras, he would win his case. Due to an overload of asylum cases, however, the officer predicted that it would take at least a year to get a court hearing. A year was likely a generous estimate. According to the American Immigration Council, in 2016, the US immigration court system was backlogged with over 620,000 cases.[24] (By 2019, that number had risen to over 800,000.[25]) Additionally, Fernando would be pursuing asylum through the defensive process, and defensive asylum seekers confront an average wait time of over three years. In some states, such as Texas, that average is five years. In contrast, those who apply for affirmative asylum wait an average of two years just for their initial interview.[26] In 2019, the average times for an asylum cases increased even further with the implementation of "Remain in Mexico" complicating the legal process for those who could still even apply.

Even without the asylum chaos wrought by the Trump administration, Fernando decided that applying for asylum was not worth pursuing. Since he had previously been caught entering the US illegally, he would likely be held in a detention center while his application was processed. As the American Immigration Council reports, immigrants "who are detained suffer mental and physical health problems including depression, post-traumatic stress disorder, and frequent infections." Furthermore, they note, "There are no statutory limits to the amount of time a non-citizen may be held in immigration detention. Some asylum applicants may be kept in immigration detention for several months or even years."[27] According to lawyer Dagmar Myslinska, immigration facilities can be very stressful for detainees, who are taken to the centers in handcuffs, are stripped of all their belongings, must wear jumpsuits, and are constantly guarded. In short, it's like being in prison, except that migrants don't even know how long they will be detained.[28]

Fernando was not willing to risk detention for the slim chance that he would receive asylum. He calculated the risks of being denied and deported. To him, they were higher than the risks of the perilous illegal journey across Mexico and the border. Not surprisingly, he opted for illegality.

By contrast, Evelia, her three daughters in tow, took the legal route, anxiously awaiting the decision that would determine their future.

After crossing the border, they ended up in a detention center. Luckily, they only had to stay there for a few days. Although brief, detention was still stressful. "They don't tell you anything. They didn't say anything, they just took some people over here and others over there," Evelia recalled. "We couldn't bathe because we didn't have any clothes. Everything you bring, they take." Inside the detention center, Evelia heard stories that only added to her distress. She mentioned one woman, who was crossing at an established point of entry with her sick son when she was detained and questioned about the medicine she was carrying for him. "Because her son was sick," Evelia asserted, "well I think it was for this reason, they didn't let them enter." Whether that was the case or not, Evelia's uncertainty highlights how those who are detained are kept ignorant of the logic or law behind the process. When left unexplained, asylum or detention becomes an indecipherable bureaucratic beast where punishments and decisions are doled out at random.

On the third day of their stay, immigration authorities were able to communicate with Evelia's cousin, and verify that he could act as her sponsor. The cousin bought airline tickets, and just like that, Evelia and her daughters were on their way out of detention. "They let us out in the middle of the night—well, who knows what time it was because inside you don't see either the day or night. Everything looks the same." Before Evelia could leave, the authorities placed a tracking device around her ankle. "And they told me not to try and take it off, because an alarm would go off . . . With that thing, they monitored where you went." Evelia recalled that when she was on the airplane, the alarm started to sound for no reason. As everyone began to stare, she frantically thumped the device until it stopped, ashamed that even as an asylum applicant following the law, she still was made to wear a device that made her feel like a criminal.

They settled with her cousin in Redmond, Oregon. However, her cousin soon moved to Portland, and while Evelia still received financial support from his family, it was difficult for her and her daughters to live on a tiny income in an area where the cost of living was skyrocketing. Fortunately, Evelia had finally been granted permission to work in the United States. The appreciation she felt to be able to work was evident on her face as she continued to emphasize, "estamos bien."

Evelia's first court date had been set for January 2018, but her lawyer explained that the judge could postpone the hearing, and that the process could take two to three years. "Nothing's certain," Evelia uttered. Her long eyelashes formed an umbrella over her downcast eyes. "Everything's in the judge's hands." If rejected, Evelia had decided that she would take her daughters and return to Mexico. "I just hope there's no problems," she added. "Because one can't really decide for themselves what they have to do." She was referring to maneuvering through the bureaucratic pipes of the immigration process. The system required Evelia to go to Eugene, Oregon every month to check in with the authorities, a six-hour round trip drive. Central Oregon's public transportation is virtually non-existent, so for someone like Evelia, without a car, the trip was complicated. "We've been doing everything correctly," Evelia offered, perhaps trying to counter the stereotypes that links illegality with Latino immigrants. "*Gracias a Dios, ahorita estamos bien.*" (We're doing well—thank God.)

As Evelia veered from memories of detention to stories about her children in the US, it became clear that her husband had not come north with the family. I asked about him, and this bubbly, gregarious woman immediately fell quiet. "I don't know, I don't know," she said, shaking her head softly. The room simmered to silence. "We came here because he disappeared." She told me he had vanished in February 2016. "And since then we haven't heard anything. It happened in Guerrero, and we still don't know anything. For a long time afterward, we looked, but we didn't find anything." Her words folded together into mumbles, kneaded closed like a ball of dough.

Evelia reported her husband's disappearance to the local authorities, but in a place where so many go missing and justice is mired in corruption, she had very little faith that anything would be done. After four months of waiting and wondering, she and her children left for the US. Still, Evelia kept hope that her husband would appear. "If something really bad happened, they find out really quickly because they identify the bodies," she offered. She gripped her thighs, her fingertips creating ten small bowls as she pressed into her muscle. "And we're okay because maybe one day he might appear, even though right now we don't have news."

"We're doing really well," Evelia added when I saw her at an event several months later, although she was still awaiting her court decision, and there was no news of her husband. As we parted ways at the end of the night, she added the same sentiment she had the last time I had seen her, "*Gracias a Dios, ahorita estamos bien.*"

PART THREE

TWENTY THOUSAND LEAGUES UNDER THE MIGRATION SEA

Three migrants wait in *El Albergue*'s patio until nightfall, due to recent changes in the shelter's rules.

Six

LA BESTIA

SEVEN-THIRTY IN THE MORNING. NORMALLY, I would just be shaking the sleep from my eyes, barely registering the familiar screech of the freight train rolling through Celaya. Over the course of my stay in Central Mexico, the freight train became another mournful sound marker in time, like the church bells that seemed to ring at a different time each day. But while the bells marked the start of a new day, the train horn announced a more enigmatic and austere truth: another wave of migrants had passed through Celaya.

The sound of the train particularly gnawed at me this morning. Instead of letting my eyelids droop for a few more minutes of sleep, I lay awake, thinking of the migrants I had met the night before at the shelter. Their faces reverberated in my mind as the morning sun filtered through the slats in the window shades. They would be leaving the shelter about now in the dampened light, the pink hues making the city look a little less harsh. From there they would head to the railroad tracks and wait until the sun peeked over the horizon and the train rumbled by. Sometimes it would stop, sometimes it would not—but either way, they would try to jump aboard. They had no choice.

"Guys have lost their legs trying to hop the train," an eighteen-year-old boy had told me the previous night, his infant son grasping at his fingers.

La bestia thunders through town.

I asked what it was like with a baby.

"We'll strap him to my back," the young man responded. "But I met a family that was going with three kids. They had to pass the kids to each other as they grabbed onto the train."

La bestia, ('the beast') as migrants call the freight trains that snake through Mexico, is an unofficial symbol of the hardships of the journey north. Before patrolling the tracks became a priority for Mexico's immigration officers, migrants would climb aboard the train wherever it came to a stop. However, once the authorities began to patrol these stops, migrants faced a stark choice: either walk across the entirety of Mexico, or jump on a train moving anywhere from twenty to sixty miles per hour. Most chose the latter.

"How do you get on a train that's moving that fast?" I asked a man who had done the journey six times, each time by train. He described it the best he could. When the beast came, he would start running alongside it. The goal was to time the rhythm of his gait with the train's movement, a calculation that seemed inexact at best. When the timing felt right, he would leap, latching onto the ladder rungs that leapfrogged to the top of the train. To avoid swinging outward, he would have to immediately reel himself into the train's rusted sides. Once he had his footing, he would scurry to the top, where he would stay for hours—or days—until the train reached the next unpatrolled stop.

But hopping the train was just one risk of the ride. What was most worrisome to many migrants were the train bandits. "They rob and assault people," one preteen boy, traveling alone, expounded. "They know we're coming and they take advantage of us, and the ones that are part of the government are trying to intimidate us. They'll shoot people just for migrating."

While many Central Americans risk their lives on the freight train lumbering north, if they are caught on the other side of the border, the return trip is often by plane. This irony was not lost on Mauricio, a recently deported emigrant from Honduras. "They treat you like a criminal, like a fugitive, like a dog," he complained. He was the most talkative member of the group, and as the conversation progressed through the evening, he leaned away from the curve of the couch and more intimately into the circle. During his plane ride back to Honduras, he was handcuffed at the ankles and wrists for the entire flight. "They gave me a sandwich, which was really just a piece of bologna and bread, and that's all I ate for the day."

"Same for me when they brought me back. Dogs eat better in your country," another young man, who had also just been deported, interjected.

"But I was handcuffed," Mauricio continued. "So, I *was* like a dog trying to eat that sandwich. I couldn't use my hands." He leaned over and imitated eating with just his mouth. The others laughed. Mauricio rocked back into the couch with a satisfied smile.

"Yeah, we like to be handcuffed," an older man with a graying beard joked, holding his pressed-together wrists in the air. "It's all a game for us."

If migration actually were a game, it would a life and death affair where "winning" meant boarding a moving train without getting maimed, killed or assaulted. And the prize for winning would be to be sent home in handcuffs, only to have to play again and again.

The eighteen-year-old with the baby was about to play again. His gaze shifted from his son squirming on his lap to the faded white wall. He spoke in uneven rhythms, issuing half-finished thoughts. He had been deported only two months before, but was going to try to cross the border again—despite having spent six months in a detention center prior to being deported. This is all he could do. Two of his sisters had died in Honduras. He couldn't stay there. "*No somos exploradores,*" he told me. "We are not explorers. We don't go to the US because we're adventurous or because we want to. We go out of necessity."

This time he would travel with the mother of his child, who was upstairs resting. The three of them were heading to Denver, to be with members of his family who lived there. I scribbled my email address on a torn-out slip of paper and told him to let me know when he made it there, the capital of my home state.

As I wrote my name on the paper, I didn't know exactly what I could do for him, in a city where I no longer lived. But somehow it seemed like one tangible thing I could offer in an otherwise entirely uncertain world.

Una tortugita que se llama Chapulín

I saw myself in those girls; it was impossible not to. They looked about three years apart in age, just like my sister and I were. The older one had dark brown straight hair, pulled together into a floppy ponytail aback her neck. Loose strands framed her tiny brown face; her hair brought back images of my sister's similarly messy buns. The younger girl was maybe three years old, and her curly hair was collected into a ponytail that sprouted from the top of her head like a piece of broccoli. Wisps of this baby hair formed delicate spirals at the edge of her forehead, and her doe-like eyes dominated her little face. They were playing in the corner of the shelter, flipping the pages of a picture book and making up stories about the wonders of the mysterious letters on the pages.

Jocelyn and María after their family moved to *El Refugio*. The family stayed in *El Albergue* for their first night in Celaya, but needed longer-term shelter so that Jacqui could give birth before continuing north.

On the other side of the room, their parents and I shared a frayed sofa. They were José Ernesto and Jacqueline, an El Salvadorian couple heading toward Houston via *la bestia*. Jacqui's belly bulged out over the top of her jeans and her shirt crept up the mound; she was eight months pregnant. The family had left El Salvador in October 2016, but had stopped in Huichipan, Hildalgo, in November so that Ernesto could work and save up enough money for the rest of the journey. He took a job working seven days a week for 120 pesos (the equivalent of six dollars) a day, and was not even paid for his work on Sundays. Nonetheless, it was a job—and that was what the family needed. They had originally expected to be assisted by Jacqui's mother in Houston upon their arrival, but they had been calling her and sending messages and hadn't heard anything back. "I think they've regretted helping us," Ernesto lamented. "Now we don't have anywhere to live."

Why would this family choose to leave El Salvador, especially when the journey is arduous even for a single male, much less for a pregnant woman and two little girls? "We're going for them," Ernesto began, glancing at the girls in the corner. "So that their future is different." And now was the time to go. The family had run out of money in El Salvador and jobs were scarce. "There where we live, it's pure coffee, pure coffee plantations." *There* referred to a rural village where Ernesto and Jacqui had spent their whole lives. However, the price of coffee had recently plummeted, forcing the plantation to cut much of its workforce, including Ernesto.

Why wouldn't Ernesto just take his family to another village or to the city and find a job there, instead of journeying all the way to a distant America? "Well the other problem is the gangs," Ernesto shared. "At least in the old days, one could go and work in another town, but not anymore . . . because the town where I live is one gang's (territory) and the town that I go to is another gang's . . . Just because I live in the other's territory, I can't go into another (gang's) territory anymore." Indeed, as chronicled in Chapter Two, economic opportunity and gang violence are intricately interlinked in countries like El Salvador, Honduras, and Mexico. "For this reason, many of us are migrating.

Because imagine if, shall we say, a guy that is from our (territory) gets his degree. He can no longer go look for a job in a factory or business in another town. Why? Because he'll go work for two or three days and then, well, the gangs will ask for his earnings. And if he doesn't want to give it to them, they will kill him. Or they say he has to become part of

Ernesto cooks dinner at *El Refugio*. He did constant volunteer work around the shelter so that his family could stay for multiple months.

the gang. Because of this, many people don't look for jobs elsewhere. They prefer to leave for the United States."

In the US, we are rooted to the idea that education and hard work spur economic opportunity. But when criminal networks have the final say, does having an education and working hard mean anything? Ernesto was right—education was worthless if you were arbitrarily limited to the jobs that existed in one gang's territory, an imaginary line that held dire consequences for your life.

Ernesto told me that the journey north was most difficult on his wife and children, but "nothing bad has happened to them so far, thank God." Tellingly, Ernesto did not consider sleeping in the street, begging for money, walking hundreds of kilometers with two (almost three) children under seven, going hungry, and taking a train that was never meant for passengers—all of which had occurred on their trek—to be "bad" things. He knew that there were a lot worse that could happen on the road north, especially to women.

The family's first attempt to leave in early October 2016 had been unsuccessful. They had crossed the Mexican–Guatemalan border, but only got as far as Tapachula, Chiapas, where the *combi* they were on was detained at a checkpoint. On their current journey to the border, they had decided not to risk the *combi* or any of the public buses, which were more likely to be patrolled by immigration authorities. Instead, they had walked across the entire state of Chiapas. Ernesto described one night when it was pouring rain and they had nowhere to sleep. The girls were soaked through their pink sweatshirts. Eventually the family came across an old abandoned car. Crawling underneath, they spent the night there, the raindrops percolating through the rust and plastering their foreheads.

"*Yo estaba temblando,*" Jocelyn, the oldest daughter, suddenly interjected. "I was trembling." I had been unaware that she had been listening to the conversation. I pictured six-year-old Jocelyn sleeping under a rusty car in the rain, and wondered what her innocent mind made of what she had already been through. Six is old enough to comprehend that the life you are living is transitory. Six is old enough to grasp that there are certain evils that even your parents can't shield you from. The rain hits your face and they can't keep you warm. At six, you recognize that it feels scary to grab the rungs of a freight train, but you're not old enough to understand why you're doing it. You carry all the emotions of the world inside you, but none of the logic.

I wondered what other emotions Jocelyn carried inside her

as the family walked for three more days, before arriving in Puerto Escondido, Oaxaca. Amidst the surf vibe of this beach vacation town, they slept in the streets and begged for money from tourists. Ernesto recalled how "a guy from your country" gave them 150 pesos (about seven US dollars), which was enough to allow them to continue north. From there, they would go by train. "Since she's pregnant, it's up to me to fight with the bags and get (the girls) on," Ernesto said. "If the train stops, we get on, but if it doesn't stop, we don't. No way." Not getting on the moving train meant that the family would often have to wait days to climb aboard, or walk even further distances. But there was no better option.

"Do you feel vulnerable?" I asked Ernesto as his wife accepted an animal sticker from her oldest daughter.

"Yes, I do." There was certainty in his words. "Because I have everything here." "Everything" was his wife, his two girls, and his unborn baby. I couldn't help but think that Jocelyn picked up on the subtleties of her own vulnerability, storing them away in layers deep within herself. What parts of this experience would she carry with her going forward? What would become the unwritten notes in the tune of her unconscious?

There are still times when the uncertain moments of my childhood arise and launch me right back into being my six-year-old self. Transitions often do the trick. Any period laced with uncertainty makes me feel just as vulnerable as the six-year-old who wasn't quite ready to move between her divorced parents' households. I would stare out the window on a Sunday night, watch a car pull up to come get me and my sister, and feel a sinking sense of losing my balance. The Sunday-night blues still come back to me often. They are a part of me, a reaction to change that I will probably never quite shake. It was impossible to pinpoint what reoccurring feelings the trip north might bring up for Jocelyn later in life. All I knew was that her six-year-old self was recording all that she passed through, weaving an emotional web somewhere in the depth of her core.

Jocelyn came over and nestled up to the base of her mother's feet. She was drawing something in her notebook—a picture of herself and her family, she explained.

"Are you leaving already?" she asked reproachfully as I tucked my notebook into my backpack.

"Not yet," I assured her.

"Want to see my drawings?" She offered me her notebook, which was plastered with butterfly stickers and scribbled figures.

"Is that you?" I pointed to a rounded drawing that had a face and some hatch marks.

She smiled, cocking her delicate neck up at me. "*¡No! Es una tortugita que se llama Chapulín.*" She giggled as she told me it's a little turtle named Grasshopper.

"Ah, that makes sense," I responded, because it did in fact look like a turtle. But, of course, drawing a turtle named Grasshopper was a piece of kid logic that would make any adult's heart turn to melted butter. What is rational to us can be bent and molded until it becomes something else entirely for a kid. I hoped the journey north could be kneaded into something softer in Jocelyn and her sister María's minds, just as a turtle could be called Grasshopper. There would always be a certain ugliness behind these days for them, a sliver of darkness and uncertainty hanging in the air they breathed. Earlier, Ernesto had described how every time the family passed a park, the girls would beg to stop and play. "Sometimes it gives me the urge to cry, or even to return," he sadly shared.

I was sure it was the same for his girls—the longing to be kids balancing unsteadily on the tumultuous ground beneath them. But I hoped, deep in my softened heart, that they would find a base of stabil-

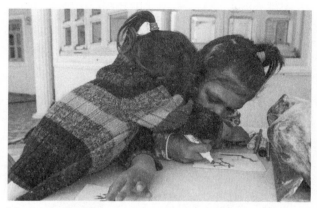

María reaches for a marker as the girls draw during a morning at *El Refugio*. The girls would entertain themselves with doodling and games, but they would inevitably bore and beg their mom to play outside the shelter.

ity one day that could ease the emotional weight of watching the train tracks pass beneath their little feet.

Seven

POLLEROS AND OTHER DELINCUENTES

DURING MY FIRST FEW MONTHS interviewing migrants at the shelter in Celaya, it was difficult to strain out an interviewee's individual experience from the more general risks of the migrant path. Migrants would often talk to me in the third person, saying "this happens and that happens," as opposed to "this happened to me." I initially believed that separating themselves from the ugliness of the passage was an attempt to depersonalize—and thus minimize—its dangerous realities. Yet as I listened to more and more stories, it became clear that this distancing wasn't some kind of psychological safety blanket, but rather a reflection of the shared vulnerability that *all* migrants bear as they head toward the border.

An integral element of this shared vulnerability is the network of both legal and illegal forces that prey upon Central Americans who transit through Mexico. These forces can be divided into five shifting and interrelated groups: cartel or gang members; the migration patrol; train security guards, *polleros* or coyotes; and random *delincuentes* (criminals). With so many groups targeting them, it is unlikely that a migrant will make it out of Mexico without being robbed, assaulted, extorted, even raped. As the migrants in the shelter told me their often harrowing stories, it became clear that the violent attacks—as well as the constant stress of not knowing who to trust on the journey north—harmed them in innumerable physical and emotional ways.

Andando Solo

He stood on the street outside the migrant shelter, and it was his clothes that made me wary. Unlike most other migrants, he was dressed nicely, wearing a black button-up shirt with white zigzags, a black skater hat that read "VANS OFF THE WALL," and a pair of clean jeans. A large diamond stud perked out of his left earlobe.

"Are you going into the *casa de migrante*?" he asked me.

I questioned whether I should check in with the staff first rather than let him enter behind me. But this hesitation faded, and we passed through the door together.

As soon as he sank into one of the couches, I could tell that he was completely exhausted. Lupita was sprawled over a chair, her legs flung over the armrest. Her tight tank top crept up to expose her love handles, and the headphones in her ears unabashedly blared music for all to hear. She tapped away at her cellphone, and cackled at the incoming texts. Once our presence registered, she lowered the volume and began to ask questions of the visitor, filling out a form without changing her posture.

"Name?"

"Fernando."

"When are you leaving?"

"Tomorrow morning at six."

"Education?"

"Elementary."

Lupita seemed satisfied by these three answers and returned to texting and blasting music.

There was no one else at the shelter, so I decided to try and talk to Fernando. He was initially reluctant to speak to me, and I had no intention of probing. Instead, I shared my *pan de muerto* with him between pockets of small talk. It quickly became clear that he did not trust me. For many on the road north, trust—or more accurately, mistrust—is a major issue, as they must weigh the benefits of trusting a stranger versus the risk of getting hurt. Can a migrant trust the person that sees them sleeping on the streets and offers a place to stay? What about police officers and other government officials? Even supposed "regular" people can turn out to be *delincuentes*—businesspeople whose avocation is exploitation.

After several pieces of *pan de muerto*, Fernando slowly started to share his story with me, perhaps because the experiences he carried inside needed to be deflated into the open air. He came from Tegucigalpa, the capital of Honduras, and this was his third time migrating. He was eighteen years old when he first left his country. He painted the dangers of his neighborhood and city in broad strokes. Tegucigalpa, he noted, is highly controlled by *pandillas,* gangs that do not hesitate to use murder, torture, and intimidation as their instruments of violence. These gangs run through the currents of everyday life, and efforts to avoid them are impossible. "In the place I live, if I want to work, they'll charge me 'rent' and if I don't pay it, they'll kill me," Fernando disclosed. A familiar story. An impossible dilemma.

"I had problems in my country. We are scared for our lives," he continued. When I pressed him about whether he had choices other than migration, he responded, "I tell you that I didn't decide to migrate. Instead it was a decision I made because I had to do it. I worked in the market, you understand? Delivering products." For a moment I thought that perhaps he was involved in the drug trade. Maybe some relationships had gone awry and he had to flee. I was very wrong. The translation was literal. "In a grocery store, my uncle's business," was where he worked. When they couldn't pay the *pandillas* the rent they demanded, Fernando and his uncle began to receive death threats. "Because of all this I decided, I have more life left to live. And with technology, you know, they figure out where you are and everything. So because of this I migrate, and I keep coming back and coming back."

When I asked what had happened to his uncle, Fernando stated blankly that he didn't want to talk about it. He looked right at me as he said this, but his eyes stared through me, as if I were just a transparent body hurling questions at him. We left the subject pending in one of the many unexplored corners of his story.

Three times heading north. Three perilous journeys, the current one half complete. Endless details. With each anecdote he shared, it felt as if Fernando was adding a piece of straw to an enormous haystack accumulating in the throes of my mind. This haystack was a conglomeration of indistinguishable migrant stories, some of them unique from the others, most of them depressingly similar. And as this pile of stories expanded, it became less and less comprehensible, harder to see the whole beyond the individual pieces. How do you make sense of the macro—the policies that create this web of violence?

Fernando had certainly experienced the violent apparatus that is the harrowing journey through Mexico. During his first trip north as an eighteen-year-old, he had been assaulted. "It was this armed guy outside the bus station," he remembered. The man kidnapped Fernando in order to demand ransom from his family. "But they let me go because I don't have any family." His voice trailed off. The closest thing to family that Fernando had was an uncle living in the States, a man he had never met and did not plan to see once he crossed the border. He also had a son back in Honduras, but he no longer spoke with the mother, and the boy lived with her. The fact that he was alone may have made him more vulnerable to being kidnapped, but, ironically, it may have also saved him, as the kidnapper concluded that there was no one to pay ransom. "Yeah . . . they left me, but nice and beat up."

During his second trip north, he had an even more harrowing encounter with *delincuentes*. "They hit me," he divulged. "They had machetes and they cut me up real nice with those machetes." Fernando had run into these bandits while waiting for the train. This assault occurred during one of the few times when he wasn't alone, instead traveling with six other migrants. At first, the group thought the criminals were just another set of migrants about to catch the train. But then they extracted their pistols and machetes and held everyone at gunpoint. Fernando was the first to get hit, and as they began to beat him, two of the other six were able to run away. Fernando and one other person remained, enduring the beating.

After Fernando was thrashed to near unconsciousness, the bandits left him and his other beaten companion, kidnapping the remaining two who hadn't escaped. For hours, Fernando floated in and out of consciousness. When he regained enough strength to take stock of his surroundings, he realized that the bandits had stolen 900 pesos (about forty-five dollars), his cellphone, watch, and a silver chain. "They took almost everything," he recalled. "They wanted to kill me, but thanks to God, I survived." The other tortured member of the group had not, his lifeless corpse draped next to Fernando as a grotesque reminder of the fate met by many others on the journey to the border. Unsure of what had happened to his other compatriots, Fernando gathered his remaining strength and limped to the nearest migrant shelter. It took six months for him to recover there.

"I don't know why these things always happen to me," Fernando lamented. "Maybe sometimes it's because of the way I dress because I know that not all immigrants dress the same." I thought about the way I had viewed Fernando when we first stood outside the migrant shelter. It was true: his gangster-like outfit had labeled him as a threat. "But I don't even have a tattoo that identifies me as a gang member." Then, referring to the way he dressed and how he might be perceived, he added, "It's my way. I can't change it." He bemoaned the fact that while migrating, he had no real way to defend himself, since he risked being perceived as a criminal by the police if he carried a gun. Thus, he could easily be overpowered by *delincuentes*. Yet when I asked if he felt vulnerable, he shot back, "Vulnerable? I don't think so," exuding the sense that although there were always risks, he was confident in his abilities. In fact, his abilities seemed to be the only thing he trusted. "I don't have anyone to help me," he added. "Just God."

After the six months spent recovering in the shelter, Fernando resumed what most consider the most difficult part of the journey: crossing the border. Like many, Fernando decided to cross the Sonoran Desert. Unlike most migrants, however, Fernando had decided to cross the desert alone. "I don't trust anyone," he offered as his reasoning.

"But don't you have a much greater chance of surviving the extreme heat, dehydration, and disorientation of the desert if you go in a group or with a *coyote*?" I asked.

Fernando confessed that he had become extremely disoriented at times during the eleven days it took him to cross the desert. During one of these confused interludes, he recollected, "I saw a hill, and I knew I had to go toward that hill. My life was in that hill." Fernando made it past this knoll but was severely dehydrated. He knew he had to make the choice that many border-crossers eventually must: ask for help from strangers, and risk being turned in. Despite his lack of trust in others, Fernando took the risk. "I asked for water from some *hermanos*, from some brothers." He smirked as he tested out the English word. "And they turned me in to law enforcement. I asked for water because I just couldn't take the thirst anymore." He returned to his dress as a possible reason for their decision. "They thought I was a bad person maybe because of the way I dressed, because I was really dirty." He glanced down at his clothing. Appearance matters. This seemed to be the implicit truth engrained in his understanding of the world.

This most recent failed attempt to cross the border had occurred five months ago. Since then, he had considered applying for political asylum, but due to the unlikelihood of receiving it, the long wait, and the strong possibility of being detained in the meantime, Fernando decided against it. He knew that his life was in danger if he returned to Honduras. His current plan was to try again to enter the US illegally. Three options: detention, risking death in Honduras, or the hazards of migrating. Migration, regardless of the numerous perils it held, was still his best choice.

This had brought him to Celaya. I asked if he would continue the journey alone again, knowing the difficulties of the desert. "Yes," he assured me. "It's difficult to travel in a group because you have to walk so far and if the train comes you have to grab it, and if you grabbed it, great, and if not . . ." His words evaporated into the empty spaces around us. Perhaps his urge to be alone had to do with what he had already experienced. A companion beaten to death. Kidnappings. Betrayal by *hermanos*.

Fernando looked up at me and to the looming silence that hung in the room, added, "Sometimes you just have to go at it alone."

Cinco veces seguiditas

"You should talk to him," the other migrants told me, gesturing to a young man tucked in the corner on a couch. "They beat him up on the train."

Freddy heals at *El Refugio*. Though not visibly battered, Freddy sustained several internal injuries when beaten by train guards.

I ambled over and sat beside him. He straightened his posture and gave me a friendly smile. Freddy was just twenty-two years old, his square face framed by thin sideburns.

"Yep, they beat me up," Freddy confirmed as soon as I sat down. He was clearly angry about the beating, though it didn't really seem to surprise him. "*Pinche guardia*," he started. Damn guards. "It's just part of it all, I guess." He then recounted the rest of the story. "They beat me in Huichapan . . . The train guards, they beat me in the ribs . . . They grabbed me at gunpoint . . . and they demanded money, but I didn't bring any. So they beat me . . . Even my teeth hurt. I put my arm up trying to defend my face, but it didn't help me. It's very dangerous out there." Even after suffering serious internal injuries in the assault, Freddy still had to walk for two days through the hills of Hidalgo, until he could take a bus that brought him to Celaya. He was then able to get a room at the city's other shelter, *El Refugio*, where migrants can stay long-term. I had started visiting this second shelter in April 2017, after I learned of its existence from Ernesto and Jacqui, who had moved there with their daughters. In this shelter, volunteers were plentiful, and the on-call doctor checked in with Freddy frequently. Although his belly was still tender, he seemed to be doing okay.

Who had beaten you, I asked? He answered that his assailants had been members of the *guardias del tren*, private security officers who roam the train tracks with paddles, looking for stowaways. When they see someone on the train who shouldn't be there, it's their job to get them off—by any means necessary. Sometimes that involves robbing or threatening migrants—or beating them nearly to death.

In addition to searching for unauthorized riders, these officers are also scouring for thieves looking to steal the train's cargo and sell it on the streets. Nayeli, a volunteer at the shelter, once mentioned an incident where thieves had punctured a car on a stopped freight train, causing corn to pour out. People from the surrounding village quietly gathered, collecting as much corn as they could. Desperation and poverty affected everyone—from the criminals trying to make a buck off corn, to local townspeople.

This was not the first beating Freddy had endured at the hands of the train guards. His first had been as the result of being mistaken for a thief. "When we came here in the train, we saw cans and metal things falling behind us, stuff that they were robbing," he recalled. "The train *guardias* arrived quickly, and the thieves went running. And we stayed there because we didn't do anything, you know . . . And since they didn't catch the people that robbed the train, they grabbed us saying that we had robbed it. But we didn't have anything to do with it. They confused us, I guess, and they beat us all."

Freddy was from the *municipio* of Jutiapa in Guatemala. Since leaving home, he'd been deported from Mexico five times, mostly from near the country's border with Guatemala. He clearly recalled each deportation—and subsequent beating. "The first time they had me get off the bus . . . From there they deported me to Tapachula to send me to Guatemala. Arriving in Guatemala, once again I crossed the border in a boat . . . I made it as far as Arriaga, once again by bus, but this time avoiding the claws of immigration. Until they beat me in Arriaga and they deported me again, to Tapachula again, and then from there to Guatemala. So after I tried out the train . . . I crossed by train and I made it to the heart of Oaxaca and there they made me get off because they caught me while I was sleeping in the train. This was the third time. They beat me, and then they deported me to Tapachula. And I tried again but this time I went in *combi*. I caught a bus directly to where God permitted me to arrive . . . in Oaxaca. Until they made me get off again. That was the last time and now enough, thank God, enough." Freddy maintained that the more times he was deported, the more "it gives me drive to keep going . . . I'm not going to be defeated. No, more like I say to myself, 'I have to make it.'"

It was not uncommon to meet migrants like Freddy—people trying for the fifth, sixth, seventh time to make it to the US. Undeterred, these migrants invest in the notion that the more they try, the more likely they are to get through. The evidence supports this. According to a study done by the Center for Comparative Studies at the University of California, out of the migrants apprehended by the US Border patrol, between 92 and 98 percent eventually get across the border, after multiple attempts.[1] These success stories become the gossip of the shelters, touted as evidence that you should keep trying. Freddy, who hadn't even made it to the US–Mexican border, carried this same unwavering conviction that he would make it through.

Freddy's family was split between the US and Guatemala. Since the age of fourteen, his parents had been going back and forth between the two countries. His father had left first, then his mother, and for a few years he lived with his grandparents. Over the course of his childhood, he told me that his father went to the States six times to work, usually staying for two or three years at a time. Freddy was used to his family being stretched across countries. "All my cousins are over there," he said. "And they're the ones I've spent the most time with . . . That's what I'm looking for—being with them . . . There are only three of us in the family that haven't gone." Not only was seeking work in America a means for Freddy to support his wife, two and four-year-old daughters, and his parents, but it also seemed to be a family rite of passage. He didn't plan to stay. Rather, he wanted to work for a few years with his cousins and then return to his wife and children. This was an experience practically everyone in his family had gone through, and "God willing," he would too. For now, he planned to take refuge at the shelter and, as the doctor had advised, recover.

As we wrapped up our conversation, Freddy rolled back and sprawled on the sofa, clutching his belly like a pregnant woman. A friend at the shelter uttered something to him and a playful smile crept across his face. Freddy had been repeatedly robbed and beaten, and deported five times, but there was still a lightness about the way he described his journey. The more they beat him down, it seemed, the more he wanted to make it.

The First Trip North

Olvin looked exhausted as he spoke. "I didn't think it was going to be like this. It's so hard. Tiring." He was migrating for the first time, and hadn't anticipated the physical and emotional adversity of the journey. His shoulders slumped inward and his head drooped. "I thought it was going to be easier because when I'd look at my friends, they would say to me 'I'm already inside!' So I would say 'oh it's easy." No it's not. A

Freddy poses by *El Refugio*'s entrance after being cleared by the shelter's doctor to continue his journey north.

person runs so many risks . . . It's something completely unexpected."

While it's unlikely that his friends had had an easy time migrating, the world of migration that Olvin was now part of was in fact changing. Donald Trump had been elected president of the United States a few months earlier, and the feared crackdown on immigration was starting to emerge. In the shelter, an ominous cloud of uncertainty hung over everyone's words and interactions. Symbolically, when I had entered that day, all the occupants were gathered in the front room, while the back room (with the bathrooms, kitchen, and beds) remained locked off. On the door, a sign read, "Knock if you need something, and maybe I'll answer," in a brazenness befitting not only of Lupita, but the overall political climate.

The ambiguity of the political situation was even more apparent at the border. I kept receiving Facebook messages from Danny, a migrant I had met a few weeks earlier, who was waiting in Sonora to cross the border. He told me that the authorities were much more vigilant than they had been before. This increased policing, however, did not deter him. He was still determined to find the right *pollero* to transport him across the most isolated and high-risk crossing point.

I looked at Olvin. He was just a few years older than me, with full black hair and a small mole accenting his forehead. During particularly stressful parts of his story, he would tilt his head and his hand would pause in the thick of his hair, pulling at the tufts with anxiety. He had left his home in Tegucigalpa, the capital of Honduras, three weeks earlier. He'd started out with a group of seventeen cousins and acquaintances, but now he traveled with just five. He was not sure what had become of the rest. They had all originally tried to cross the Mexico-Guatemalan border together, only to be stopped by the Mexican police, who demanded 500 pesos from each member of the group. They were short on money, but after pooling their resources, the police let them through. With almost no money left, the group split up. Left alone, Olvin caught the infamous *bestia*.

"The train makes me really nervous," he confided as he picked at the edge of the table. "It comes so fast." He had experienced a close call with the train near a key migrant stopover often referred to as La Lechería. "That day—actually it was night. I was getting on the train and when I went, I couldn't grab it that well. I grabbed the last train rung, but if God were not there with me, the train would have cut my feet off, because it did take my shoe. And I don't know how I placed my feet down to be able to climb up. It was God there." He made brief eye contact before looking down at the table again. "And when that happened, my heart went boom, boom, boom." He freed a nervous chuckle. "Any other questions?"

"Do you feel vulnerable migrating?" I asked tentatively.

He bit his lower lip in what seemed to be something between hesitation and a desire to share. "Well, twice I've ended up by myself, only to find my friends further along. There was a time when I basically decided to turn myself in, but it seemed like they didn't want me to turn me in." He described how he was walking near La Lechería when he encountered the police. At that point, he was about ready to give up and return to Honduras. "But they were good police and they helped me. I told them to turn me in to *la migra*. But instead they just gave me fifteen pesos to take a *combi*." He called his mother that night, still unsure of whether he should continue on his journey. "It made me want to cry. I said, 'Mamá, I can't keep going, I want to turn myself in.'" After some encouragement from his mother, he pushed onward and eventually reunited with some of his cousins.

I could literally see the toll that migrating was taking on Olvin. It manifested in the quaver in his voice when he talked about ending his journey north, and the way he drew his biceps inward in an embryonic self-hug. He did not want to be doing this, but his only options were either heading toward the border, or the unending violence back home.

"In the *colonia,* the neighborhood where I live, it's one of the most risky and dangerous," he shared. He was referring to Colonia Villa Franca in Tegucigalpa. Honduras (particularly Tegucigalpa) has one of the highest murder rates in the world. Olvin described how his grandfather was at a bar one night in 2010 when armed gang members arrived, threatened him, and eventually fatally shot him. "I'm just so tired of so much violence," Olvin said in a weary tone.

Just a few weeks before leaving, Olvin had had his own encounter with violence. "I was walking down the street listening to music, and then the police arrived there. A really corrupt police—well, all the police are corrupt—and they say 'don't move!' I stopped and they wanted to take away my cellphone. I didn't let them take my cellphone away, so they put me in the police car, took me to the station, and put me in a cell . . . I didn't know why. The police acted like it was nothing." Olvin stretched his wrists across the table so that I could see the marks from the handcuffs. "And then they beat me. They beat me like they wanted to kill me, I don't know. They put a bag over my head so I couldn't breathe. They grabbed me right here by the Adam's apple." He wrapped his palms around his neck to imitate the chokehold. "And when I swallow, it hurts. I don't know if it's still swollen or something."

His little sister had become extremely upset when he relayed the episode. "'Don't leave the house anymore,' she pleaded. 'The police are going to take you again.' But I'm a barber. I had to work. So when I would leave, my sister would follow me and beg me to come back into the house." I could only imagine how worried his sister must be now that he was gone.

"I still don't know why they took me," Olvin continued. "I don't know, maybe like Trump, they think we're all . . ." He paused. "Or maybe they confused me with someone else, I don't know." As Olvin took a moment to process his thoughts, I thought about what it must be like to be so young and have your rights continuously eroded by violence.

The next morning, Olvin and his remaining cousins were planning to venture to Irapuato (the next train outpost), this time by taxi (Celaya's immigration patrol had become much more vigilant about monitoring the train). They would remain on *la bestia* until they reached the border, where Olvin's uncle would send money for a *pollero* to guide them across the desert. If all went as planned, Olvin would join his uncle in San Francisco before Trump clamped down further on the border. While Olvin may have imagined that the journey north would be easier, he had no delusions about life in the US as an undocumented migrant. "It's not going to be anything easy, I think. You always suffer . . . from depression or fear. I don't think it's going to be anything to enjoy."

The difficulty of living in a foreign land would be underscored by the absence of his family. "Was it hard to leave your family?" I inquired. This was the only point in our conversation where Olvin was on the verge of tears. "Ugh, still," he sighed. "I miss them. Mostly my little sister and my mom. I miss them a lot. Even when I remember it, it gives me something here." He ran his fingers along his throat, the same spot where the police had choked him a month earlier. "It's hard."

We sat in silence for a moment, the sun sinking through the room's small glass window. Finally, he said, "But I've always wanted to be able to help my *mami*. She's always dreamed of having a house there, her own house. So I wanted to reach that dream that my mom has."

As our conversation waned, we returned to the uncertain future.

Would Trump stop immigration? I asked Olvin.

"No, I don't think so. Even if he builds a wall, there will always be a place where one can pass through . . . Nothing difficult."

The *Pollero* Spectrum

On a Tuesday in May 2017, David was deported back to Querétaro. The following Friday, we arranged to meet up in a local park on the city's industrial outskirts. The busy streets, the smell of exhaust fumes, and the vendors selling everything from cheap cellphone cases to *tacos de tripas* reminded me more of Celaya than the well-kempt colonial vibe of downtown Querétaro.

As children dangled from the jungle gym and their parents relaxed on nearby benches, a man tentatively approached. He looked to be in his early twenties, and wore a sleek navy blue button-down shirt. His shaven head housed only a neatly-trimmed lawn of black hair that formed a widow's peak on his forehead. A few prickly hairs sprouted around his jaw line. This had to be David. As he settled beside me, resting his palms atop his faded blue jeans, I imagined how surreal he must have felt to be meeting an American stranger in a familiar park, just three days after being deported.

This had been David's third attempt to cross the border. A year and a half prior to our meeting, he had come to the decision that if he wanted to earn enough money for his family to survive, he needed to leave Querétaro. "The money just didn't last," he told me, "and there's just no opportunity here." With two children and aging parents, the pressure to provide for his family was immense. He had worked various jobs—from package delivery to police work—but it was "never enough." Since Querétaro is one of the safest cities in Mexico and consistently ranked among the best places to live in the country, the cost of living has steadily increased. The city's popularity and spiraling expense made it even more challenging for David to support his family. So, in 2015, he applied for a worker's visa, aiming to save up some money in the US for a few years, then return to Querétaro. Unfortunately, his visa request was rejected without explanation. However, the plan lingered in the back of his mind, fueled by the gnawing reality of the conditions around him. To enable his family to stay in the city they loved, David

David, back in Querétaro.

decided to leave and cross the border illegally.

In the media, we tend to romanticize the desolate harshness of the border. It's easy to watch a character from one of the countless border TV shows in a shootout with *narcos* and be drawn to this sense of almost spiritual mysticism in the lawlessness of the remote. But as David textured my images of the border with his words, the reality was anything but romantic or mystical.

"We were in a hotel room. The *pollero* had us locked in there for eight days," he shared about his most recent attempt to get into the US. *Polleros* (also known as coyotes), are the human traffickers who, for a hefty fee, will supposedly help migrants cross the border. The word *pollero* literally translates to "chicken wrangler," which means that their unfortunate followers become the *pollos,* or chickens. Like a slick salesman, these opportunists often connect with migrants in their hometowns, offering to safely shepherd them across the border. Once in America, the migrants are told by the *pollero* that they will be able to earn five, ten times as much as they could ever earn at home. The price for this good fortune? Just a "small sum" (several thousand dollars). After just a few years in the US, the migrant will be able to return to their family, a wealthy man or woman. With such a compelling pitch, Central Americans will frequently borrow money from friends, family—even the *pollero* himself—to fund their journey north.[2]

There is a spectrum of types of *polleros*. First, there's the local *pollero*—the aforementioned recruiter who approaches people in their hometowns when they are first considering heading north. In the scheme of things, he is probably the best—or more accurately, the least worst—kind of *pollero*. He may personally know his clients and their families, and may actually care about their survival. He is often the *guía,* (guide) who will ride, eat, and sleep with his *pollos*. Before the Zetas and other cartels co-opted the migrant world, these local guides could operate independently without working for a larger network along the border. This is not the case anymore. As journalist Óscar Martínez notes, "The good coyote no longer has that option—to be a good coyote. Instead he has to pay his dues to Los Zetas, or hand over human loot instead."[3] Indeed, even those *polleros* who don't want to be connected to the cartels have to pass through their territory, and to do so, must at the very least pay taxes for every *pollo* they help to cross. Martínez interviewed one *pollero* who was still trying to avoid working directly for the Zetas. When Martínez pressed why, the *pollero* responded

> . . . Because it's all fucked. It's not as simple as working *with* them and crossing people whenever you want. They control you. They want your home phone number back in Honduras, and they call you once in a while to cross groups they've reserved for you. If you take too long in the crossing, or if they don't see you on the road for a month, they'll fuck you over. They'll think you're working for someone else, or that you've found another crossing point. They want you to watch routes for them, they want you to get them people (to kidnap).[4]

In addition to the local *polleros* who pay dues to the Zetas and other cartels, there are also the commercialized *polleros* who are *narco* employees. Directly embedded within the violence of the cartels, these *polleros* transport large groups of migrants from *guía* to *guía* through the underground pipeline of human smuggling. Unlike the local *polleros*, the cartel-employed *polleros* could care less if their *pollos* are abandoned; in fact, they frequently turn their *pollos* over to kidnappers. As many migrants explained to me, it was hard to tell which *pollero* worked for the cartels, and which just answered to them. With everyone under *narco* control, perhaps it didn't really matter.

At least with the local and the cartel-linked *polleros*, the migrants are the ones paying the guides. There are also *polleros* who pay for bodies—criminal middlemen who corner migrants into becoming sex workers, drug mules, or kidnapping victims. As an example, these *polleros* may pay the owner of a Guatemalan brothel for migrants that they will then take north and sell to an American pimp.[5] Or they may bribe the director of a migrant shelter to hand over Central Americans, whom they then fork over to kidnappers for a cut of the ransom. When someone is paying for bodies—commodifying human lives—the illicit journey north becomes even more embedded in horrendous and relentless violence.

David wrestles with his next
move at a Querétaro park.

La Organización and the Border

Because of the frequent stories of *polleros* abandoning their clients, many migrants initially take on the journey through Mexico without a guide, relying only on their wits and tidbits of passed-down knowledge. And yet, as they wind their way north through the bowels of Mexico, there comes one defining line where most migrants have no choice but to solicit a *pollero*—the border.

One common theme that emerged during my migrant interviews was that the border is the most feared part of the journey. The trains and assaults and robberies, as harrowing as they are, are merely a preamble to a lawless territory controlled by organized crime and filled with harsh environmental hazards that can end a human life in mere days.[6] Because of the many dangers, most migrants have no choice but rely on *polleros* to get them across the border.

On top of the physical misery of the desert, migrants often get caught in the thorny relationship between *polleros* and the cartels. It is virtually impossible to cross the US–Mexican border illegally without coming into contact with cartel *narcos*, whether directly or indirectly. For most migrants, the best-case scenario is that the *pollero* pays off the *narcos*, allowing the group to continue on without incident. If the *pollero* doesn't work for the cartel and tries to sneak through without paying up, however, he and the group become targets. *Narcos* and their hit men love to teach rogue guides a lesson by assaulting, murdering, and raping their *pollos*.

Despite the threats of organized crime, it is often in a migrant's best interest to find a *pollero* who works directly for the cartels; that way, the *narcos* are less inclined to demand huge quotas, or even kill once the group crosses into their border territory. At the same time, relying on guides connected with *narcos* carries its own potential risks, as they may force the migrant to traffic drugs, or just abandon them in the desert. While migrants try their best to choose *polleros* who have the necessary connections to shield them from cartel violence, there is no guarantee that the *pollero* will have any interest in making sure their *pollos* remain safe, or alive—the money is theirs no matter what happens. "There's just no certainty," David said as we discussed the bleak nature of this dilemma. In the end, his cousin had given him the name of a *pollero* who was linked to the cartels. Better to accept that they ruled the borderlands, David figured, and hope that they let him cross safely.

As David relayed his three attempts to cross the border, his journeys melded together into one long nightmare. Each time, the *pollero* kept David and his group locked away in a hotel. No one knew when they would be leaving, and they were rarely given anything to eat. Then—after many agonizing days of starving and waiting—the *pollero* would suddenly show up and take the group to the edge of the Río Grande. Once there, they would wade through the mud of the riverbed, plunge into the tumultuous currents, and do their best to swim across.

During their first try, David and his group walked for two days through the desert after crossing the Río Grande, before *la migra* caught them. The second time, they were detained just after crossing the border. On the most recent attempt a few days before we spoke, the *pollero* abandoned the group 100 meters after crossing the river. He claimed he had to check on the group's ride, disappeared and never came back. David knew they were on their own as soon as the guide left, but what could he have done to stop him? He was powerless, compelled to put his life in the hands of someone he knew he could not trust. After a few hours of waiting for him to return, David's group accepted their fate. With nowhere to turn but north, they picked up their one-gallon water jugs and continued on through the severe desert washes without the guide they had paid to take them. After hours of leaving circles of footprints in the pulverous soil—and with their food and water supplies quickly dwindling—they were picked up by the authorities. Seeing *la migra* was a double-edged sword in this case; it meant deportation, but at least they wouldn't die in the desert.

The first time he was caught, David "voluntarily" returned home, choosing not to wait for a deportation trial. The second time, he was held in a detention center for two days while his hearing date passed, before being deported. This last time, David did not even receive an immigration hearing, since his case fell under the Trump administration's then-new expedited removal plan, which stated that immigrants caught within 100 miles of the border who had been in the US for less than two weeks could be immediately deported. Since he had attempted to cross so many times, David was now prohibited from applying for legal reentry for five years. If he were to be caught crossing illegally again, he would face imprisonment. David had decided he couldn't take that risk: he would not be returning to American soil.

Whether he was deported or returned voluntarily, the process was the same for the David. He would be dropped on the Mexican side of the border, and then it was up to him to make his way back home. This left him vulnerable to the cartels and other criminal forces along the border. "I know how things are there with organized crime. *La organización* is checking who they're returning," he shared, referring to the cartels, gangs, and the rest of the illicit migration world. They wait in border town bus stations, he told me, searching for deportees who have no opportunities, no resources, and no money. Then they offer them two choices: some sort of exploitive position with the cartel (which often can't be refused without consequences), or assault and extortion.

"I was afraid they were going to make me cross again," David stated. Why would *narcos* make migrants cross the border again, I asked. He told me there were two reasons: to force resource-poor migrants to traffic drugs, or to kidnap and detain them until their families in the States paid an absurd ransom, as had occurred with Fernando. Aware of these dangers, David decided to go directly to the *Instituto Nacional de Migración* (the government agency that controls migration) in Tamaulipas. Despite the agency's notorious corruption, which will be discussed in chapter nine, they were still his best hope for getting home. Although his request for bus money from the Querétaro office went unanswered, the Institute did help slightly by transporting him to the local migrant shelter. At the very least, he wouldn't spend his first couple of nights back in Mexico on the streets. When his family scraped together enough money to wire him the funds for a bus ticket, David headed back to Querétaro.

The few days since his return had been trying for David. "You come back without work, without money." He glanced down, pausing as if trying to recognize his own voice. "You come back with your mind like . . . oh I couldn't do it." He looked up again. Facing his family after what felt like three major failures was demoralizing. He told me he would look for work in Querétaro again, trying to piece together some kind of income. He slouched until his chest became a cavern. "You go with the illusion of getting ahead." That idea, he added, was gone now.

We gathered our things to part, leaning in for the standard kiss on the cheek. "Can I use your real name?" I asked as we meandered toward the bustling street.

"Yeah you can." He flashed me a smile. "Just as long as you don't have any links to the cartel."

Eight

THE NEW CARTEL INDUSTRY: KIDNAPPING

"THE MORE I TOLD THEM I didn't have (any money), the more they tortured me," Abrahám recalled. A Honduran man in his early twenties, he wore a purple-and-white trucker hat on his head and an expression of utter defeat on his face. When he moved through the shelter, his gait was slow and deliberate, his right leg dragging behind. The skin above his eye stretched unnaturally over his facial bones, and the remains of a wound arched up from the edge of his mouth, only slightly obscured by a short beard.

Less than a month before our conversation, Abrahám had endured three days of terror after being kidnapped en route to the United States. He'd left Honduras in December, crossed through Guatemala, and made it as far north as Veracruz. He was on top of *la bestia* when all hell broke loose. "They threw me off," he recollected, referring to members of the drug cartel, the Zetas. "And when they threw me off, more were waiting below, with bats and rocks and guns. And they said to me, 'You Honduran son of a . . .'" His voice trailed off. "And then the first thing they did was tie me up here and here." Abrahám motioned to his neck and arms. "Why the arms? Because the arms are your only defense."

The men then took Abrahám to an abandoned house, where he spent three days in a dark room. His kidnappers occasionally gave him water or shoved a cookie in his mouth. Eventually, they began to demand money. Abrahám had nothing on him and refused to provide information about his family in the US. "I have family there, but I told them I didn't," Abrahám said, adding that even if his family had sent money, there was no way of knowing if the kidnappers would have released him. "So I told them I didn't have anything and they began to beat me." The men smashed his face with their pistols and kicked at his belly like a soccer ball. But the most visceral pain came from a splinter of wood imbedded in his right thigh. When Abrahám was pushed off the train, he had fallen with such force that a stick pierced his quadricep. "They didn't take it out. It was in my leg for three days, and they used it to torture me." He described how his kidnappers would twist the stick or move it back and forth like a saw ripping apart the flesh from inside.

The hours and days became a blur of beatings and intense agony, and Abrahám began to doubt that he would get out alive. However, on the third day, he heard one of his kidnappers say, "This one is a waste of time." Just like that, he was set free. Bruised and battered, the stick still embedded in his leg, Abrahám walked for two hours until he arrived at a house. "The first house I came to helped me, but I didn't let them take out the stick because it hurt," he said matter-of-fact. "It was rotting inside." Abrahám spent fifteen days in the local hospital, where they removed the stick, cleaned the hole in his leg, and stitched up his wounds.

"I just felt so sad, so . . . well, in a word, *alone*," Abrahám confessed when describing his time in the hospital. "Because apart from the fact that I didn't have anyone, I didn't have a way to pay the hospital." In the end, the woman at the house who originally came to his aid paid his hospital bills. The charge totaled 1,500 pesos (about $75).

"Not everyone is bad," Abrahám offered as he hugged a couch pillow in toward his chest. "I say this because not everyone would have done that favor for me."

Return to the Shadows

Everyone at the shelter had heard the stories—seventy-two migrants kidnapped in Tamaulipas, fifty-three taken in Nuevo León, dozens more in Tenosique, Arriaga, La Lechería. All Central American, all abducted in places the migrants in the shelter would likely pass through on their way north. They all recognized that the kidnappings were not random, but were the product of a highly organized criminal apparatus orchestrated by the Zetas.

Why had Mexico's most sinister drug cartel branched out into extorting Mexico's most vulnerable? According to journalist Óscar Martínez, the Zetas' kidnapping operation had originally been a way to keep *polleros* in line.[1] In addition to relying on them to cross the border, many migrants also employ *polleros* for the entire journey north, traveling with them in groups from their home country and stopping in "safe houses" along the way. Because *polleros* transit through territories controlled by cartels, they either incur a cartel tax or work directly for the *narcos* in order to pass through safely. Even those who transport Central American migrants through southern Mexico have to pay this tax, or else they will be targeted by local *delincuentes* who work for the Zetas specifically to ensure that *polleros* pay up. A shelter employee in Tenosique (a town along Mexico's southern border) stated that the kidnappings "started as something against the *polleros* who didn't pay. They'd take away their *pollitos*, their little chicks. And since they already had them in their hands, they figured they'd go ahead and get a ransom from their families in the US through a fast deposit from Western

Union. And then it got to be a habit. They started picking up any migrant who walked alone."[2]

Other than to control *polleros*, why would the Zetas—a cartel that makes billions from the drug industry—trifle with kidnapping destitute travelers? There are several reasons. The first is purely economic. As the Zetas battle other major cartels for territory, diversifying their industries helps them to maintain dominance.[3] With their militaristic operation, the Zetas have the power to abduct hundreds of migrants at a time. As an Insight Crime report puts it, "If (the Zetas) already have the men, guns, vehicles, safe houses, and help of the authorities, why wouldn't they enter into kidnapping?"[4] Despite the fact that migrants have very little money, kidnapping them has proven profitable, as the Zetas primarily target their victims' families north of the border, seeking ransom. As a result, the migrant kidnapping industry in Mexico generates an estimated $250 million dollars annually.[5] As Óscar Martínez writes, "The business logic is simple: it's more profitable to kidnap forty people over a few days that will pay 300 dollars each in ransom, than it is to kidnap a businessman that will pay off the ransom, but who might alert the press or the police."[6] The Zetas hold their victims in remote ranches, charging an average of $2500 per head for their release.[7]

Beyond the money, the Zetas abduct migrants because they know they can get away with it. Migrant travelers on the road are easy to spot, and they rarely report crimes, as fear of being detained or deported typically prevents them from coming forward. Before reforms passed in 2010, there wasn't even a legal avenue for undocumented people to report crimes, as individuals had to prove their legal status in Mexico before authorities could process their allegations. Even when this requirement was scrapped in 2010, the reforms did not preclude officials from taking someone's legal status into consideration when handling their complaint.[8]

Even when undocumented people do report crimes, the authorities almost never investigate.[9] Although seven states in southern Mexico have established special prosecutor's offices to investigate migrant abuse, jurisdictional issues still impede investigations.[10] For instance, if a kidnapping occurs in Chiapas but is reported in Oaxaca (as often occurs), the dearth of coordination between state offices means that the crime will likely go unsolved. At the federal level, there is an office called the Unit for the Investigation of Crimes for Migrants within the Attorney General's Office, which was created in 2015 to investigate federal crimes (including offenses along *la bestia* and federal highways). However, the unit's offices are located far from areas where crimes typically occur, and questions over jurisdiction also delay investigations.[11] Due to these obstacles and other corruption issues in Mexico's justice system, only 1 percent of crimes against migrants in Mexico result in a conviction.[12] As a representative of the National Commission of Human Rights (NCHR) commented, "The Mexican government is supposed to be responsible for the safety and the lives of those who are in its territory. It's incredible that this is continuing to happen."[13]

In addition to grossly inadequate investigation protocols, Mexican authorities have also been accused of actually participating in migrant abductions. A 2009 report by the NCHR highlighted that out of the 10,000 kidnappings that the commission documented, "The participation of Mexican authorities in the kidnapping of at least ninety-one migrants reveals that there exists linkages between these crimes and agents of the state."[14] In another ninety-nine cases, migrants reported that they witnessed police in contact with their captors.[15] The Zetas know that they can count on the authorities to either assist in the kidnappings or look the other way, leaving no consequences for expanding this sordid operation.

While the Zetas' kidnapping trade has undoubtedly intensified over the past few years, exact numbers remain elusive. Mexico's Instituto Nacional de Migración (INM), the agency in charge of regulating immigration in Mexico, did not even track migrant abductions until 2012.[16] However, in 2009, a unit within the NCHR in Mexico conducted an investigation into migrant kidnapping in the state of Veracruz, a territory controlled by the Zetas. In just six months, they logged 10,000 cases, claiming that if they had a bigger staff, that number would have been double or triple.[17]

Once the INM began tracking kidnapping cases, the numbers still paled in comparison to the NCHR's figures. In 2013, the INM only recorded sixty-two cases, which is unsurprising given the many challenges to reporting previously mentioned. However, in 2014, the INM documented 682 cases of migrant kidnappings.[18] These victims were exclusively Central American—365 from Honduras, 200 from El Salvador, 100 from Guatemala and seventeen from Nicaragua.[19] The significant rise in documented abductions in 2014 likely reflected a combination of factors. First, the increase corresponded to a surge in unaccompanied Central American minors traveling through Mexico, who were even more vulnerable to cartel capture. Additionally, the majority of these cases occurred in Tamaulipas, Guerrero, and Michoacán, all of which were experiencing a fracturing of cartels in their respective areas. When cartels splinter, they almost always compete for territory and money, potentially sparking a spike in kidnapping.[20] The upturn could also be tied to the INM's improved efforts to document such crimes.

In 2015, Mexico's Attorney General's Office created the previously cited unit focused on investigating migrant crimes, as well as a mechanism for family members outside of Mexico to report crimes committed against their relatives.[21] In turn, the numbers continued to swell, with 707 abductions recorded in 2017.[22] While increasing reportage of these crimes is certainly a step in the right direction, the fact remains that hundreds, if not thousands, of migrants beyond the reported cases fall victim each year.

As the Trump administration pressures Mexico into ramping up immigration security, the number of kidnappings will likely increase. When common migrant routes are blocked by increased security and vigilance, migrants are forced to transit through more remote, dangerous areas. As Rubén Figueroa, an activist with the group Movimiento Migrante Mesoamericano, observes, "The new routes derived from the operations of the National Migration Institute aimed at stopping migrants cause them to transit through zones controlled by organized crime."[23] Under Trump, this trend is increasingly evident. With more security forces along the southern border and associated train routes, migrants are forced into cartel territory, and in the process, crawl into the mouth of an even crueler beast.

In May 2019, President Trump stooped to geopolitical bullying to get Mexico to act, giving new President Andrés Manuel López Obrador forty-five days to prove that he would stem the flow of Central Americans by threatening a 5 percent tariff on all goods imported from Mexico if the administration did not comply. With Mexico's economy so intertwined with that of the US, López Obrador was forced to act or risk bearing the political costs of a tanking economy. Mexican officials therefore promised to take "unprecedented steps to increase enforcement to curb irregular migration," including deploying 6,000 members of the newly formed National Guard across the country to police migrants.[24]

As a result, there has been a shift along Mexico's southern border, with armed forces and National Guard troops heedfully patrolling. Óscar Martínez reported on this increased security from the eastern sector of the country's southern border, near the kidnapping center of Tenosique, Tabasco. Within just fifty kilometers of Tenosique, Martínez observed ten municipal, federal and military checkpoints. (Prior to the agreement between Mexico and the US, there had been none.) This enhanced vigilance trickles down to even taxi and bus drivers. As one driver noted, "Migration officials threaten us if we pick up migrants. They take away our licensing."[25] This has caused taxi and bus drivers to require identification for people boarding local public transport, even though they do not have the legal authority to do so. Without public transport options, migrants are compelled to walk through isolated areas. "The message from Mexico is now clear," Martínez remarks. "Travel like migrants all your life, hidden in the mountains, not in a caravan strengthened by the highway. Return to the shadows."[26]

Of course, the shadows are where most kidnappings occur. Although the INM's 2018 and 2019 figures have not yet been released, at the local level, there has been an apparent rise in migrant assaults concurrent with the increased security. For example, the local migrant shelter in Tenosique registered 166 assaults against migrants in January 2019 alone. (In January of the previous year, the shelter only reported fifty-eight cases of assault.) Additionally, between January and February of 2019, the shelter documented 203 robberies, three kidnappings and seven instances of rape. All of these abuses reportedly happened in either rural towns, at the train tracks, or at the municipal trash dump outside the city.[27] As Martínez notes, "Just as the United States government understands that the desert will do its part to prevent migration, Mexico's government seems to know that the jungle will do its part if they close off the highway."[28] Yet "preventing" migration does not mean that migrants will not persevere. It just means that they'll suffer—or die—trying.

After his harrowing kidnapping, Abrahám returned to the shadows of the journey *al norte*. He did not speak to his parents or four-year-old daughter (who lived together in Honduras) for over a month. When he finally got in touch, his mother was extremely worried, so Abrahám decided not to trouble her further by telling her what had really happened. "I told them I had an accident. I didn't tell them how."

With his wounds slowly healing, Abrahám decided to trudge onward. Since his injuries made walking arduous, he decided to take the train. But it wasn't long before he regretted that decision. He was on top of a thirty-car train when another band of armed kidnappers clambered aboard. He could tell they were *Zetas* by the way they dressed, and how they snaked across the train cars combing for victims. "The only one that was on the train was me," Abrahám recalled. His heart began to race. "I heard them and I hid myself in a hole in one of the railcars . . . I was praying to God that they didn't see me." As he listened to the echoes of footsteps on the car above him, he kept praying. He held his breath. He tried to slink away from the sunlight leaking through the railcar hole to obscure his body. He waited. All the while he thought, *this can't be happening again.*

It took a few chilling minutes, but eventually the kidnappers' voices retracted into faint echoes until they were gone. At the next stop, Abrahám got off. It was not worth the risk to take the train. He continued on foot, dragging his right leg across dusty roads and over barren hills for fifteen days until he reached Celaya.

The horrors that Abrahám had experienced (thus far) on the journey north were not limited to what he had personally endured. Before he was kidnapped, he had watched bandits rape a Central American teenager beside the teeth of the train tracks. "They abused this woman in plain day," he said, shrinking into the pillow he cradled in his lap. "We were going in a group of various immigrants, but I'm telling you, we couldn't do anything because all of them had guns. They abused her, they abused her, in a public place. Well, not exactly in a public place, but by the train with various immigrants around." He receded into the pillow, folding like a book closing shut.

I tried to put myself in that hot afternoon scene. I imagined the dust that lined the tracks, the bits of plastic and strands of grass and rusted metal. A desolate space where violence goes unnoticed. And then a gang of armed men, their guns pointed upward, expressions hardened like the permanency of dried clay. What would I do? Like Abrahám, I would likely freeze because in this barren setting where human survival goes against the odds, you do what you have to in order to survive.

Then Abrahám added a chilling statement. "The advantage that a woman has is that they can abuse her and they leave her alive." I wrapped my mind around this horrific logic, thinking about the rotting rut of trauma that a woman who has been raped has to live with for the rest of her life. Could this ever be considered an advantage? It was a question I couldn't answer, as I had never had my body pressed against the prongs of the train tracks, with something inside me being ripped away. Abrahám provided the answer: "The disadvantage of a man is that if you don't give them (what they want), they kill you." When your other option is death, rape could be considered an advantage.

After hearing the physical and emotional misery that Abrahám had experienced on his migrant journey, I asked him why he had left Honduras in the first place? Like many migrants, it was because of economic opportunity. "Now that I have a daughter, I have to fight for her," he said, a certain intensity laced within his words. The mother of his child had left after his daughter was born, so the responsibility for caring for her fell on Abrahám, with help from his parents. "My girl eats, she needs clothes, and now she's started school," he said, explaining how all this cost money that he didn't have. He began to describe how smart his daughter was and how he wanted to feed that curiosity by continuing her schooling. "It's like the conversation I'm having with *tú, vos, usted,*" he stated, chuckling over how exactly to address me. "When my daughter doesn't understand, she keeps looking at me in the eyes and she says, 'Explain it to me better.' She's very curious."

Abrahám was ultimately unsure where he would end up. Maybe Miami Beach, where some of his brothers lived, but then he added, "My intention is not necessarily to go to the border. My intention is to stay wherever I find the first job." Abrahám had some technical training in refrigeration and had worked as a chef. But employment stability was non-existent in Honduras. "Maybe you find a job for three or four days," he explained. "But if you have a week of work, you have two or three weeks without work." Sustaining himself, his daughter, and his aging parents without consistent work was impossible, so he had to look elsewhere. "The only way to work is if you've graduated. There's just not sufficient employment. And because of this, Central Americans are going crazy trying to find work." He noted that at each stop along the journey, he looked around to see if he could find a job. He would do the same before leaving Celaya. Thus far, he had found nothing, and therefore thought that crossing the border might be necessary.

So to find a job, any job, Abrahám had left his daughter in the quiet drizzle of a winter morning. "She didn't want me to migrate. She cried." He remembered that she had asked him if he was coming back soon. "And I lied to her. I said 'yes.'" Abrahám did plan on returning to his family in Honduras, but only after he had made enough money to avoid worrying whenever he couldn't find work. "The love for a child is bigger than anything else," he told me, sitting up a little straighter and brightening as he spoke. "Yes, I dream of seeing my little girl again someday."

If he couldn't find work in Celaya (which was unlikely for someone without a Mexican ID), he planned to continue on *la bestia,* despite swearing he would never take that risk again. He felt he now had more knowledge and would therefore be more alert to potential dangers. He shared with me two strategies for his journey forward: "Migrants have to bring limes with them," he rationalized. "Because a lime, even when you haven't eaten, gives you strength. It lifts stress. It gets rid of tiredness . . . The lime is the method to secure your destiny."

Abrahám's second strategy for the journey ahead was more tactical. He planned to buy a cellphone, not to make calls, but to hand over to potential kidnappers as ransom. "If you're a migrant and you don't have money, it helps so that they let you go free." He lamented that if he had a cellphone before, he may never have been kidnapped.

After speaking for three hours, I gathered my things to go. Before I left, Abrahám remarked that during his whole journey, he had never had anyone to talk to. He hadn't told anyone about the kidnapping or the rape or the fears that festered inside him. He never knew who he could trust, who might be scouting for a *coyote* or be an informant for kidnappers. "I haven't encountered anyone where I can say, 'I'm going to tell you my story.' So thanks to *vos, tú, usted,* because to you listened to me, and listening is good. It alleviates it all."

On my walk home, I thought about to the warmth of our connection. It was not because we knew each other well—we had only spent an evening together. Rather, it was a connection based on mutual exchange. Abrahám had given me an enormous sense of respect for him and for all those that, despite hardship, pick themselves up and relentlessly believe in something better. And during a time marked by racist political discourse and a lack of understanding and compassion, I hoped that in return I had provided him a space for sharing, a space where, for once, he was truly heard.

Nine

LOS CENTROAMERICANOS Y LA MIGRA MEXICANA

MY APARTMENT COMPLEX IN CELAYA marked a dividing line between two neighborhoods. On one side, there was the Alameda, an area marked by French cuisine, coffee shops, bridal stores, a yuppie gym, and lighter skinned people strolling the streets. Barrio Zapote on the other side, however, was "kind of sketchy," as a friend put it. To the east of the apartment complex was one set of train tracks, to the north another. The eastern tracks divided the sketchy Barrio Zapote from the most dangerous neighborhood in the city, while the northern tracks denoted the line where the meandering families licking their ice cream cones would stop walking.

The northern tracks were partially fenced off from the courtyards of the houses in the Alameda; slipping through the holes in the fence, you entered a sooty world of rusted iron. A few faded grass mounds rose from the slats in the tracks, but otherwise the landscape was a field of dust. When the wind swished through, dirt would cover your lips in a thin film. Plastic bags remained entangled between each remaining blade of grass as if they were an integral part of nature. Chip bags, candy wrappers, banana peels, and plastic cups complemented the dust in a mosaic of desolation.

I would often take my regular morning run here. Above, halted freight trains carried mounds of long rectangular cement pillars, remind-ing me of the Cuisenaire rods I learned how to count with as a child. A lone rusted streetlight arched up and over the tracks. I often wondered how this picture would appear at night, when the light would drench the weary travelers in an orange hue. I could only wonder, though, for I would never venture near the tracks at night.

Crossing the tracks.

At a point where the space between the tracks and the fence narrows, I slip back to the Alameda side. It is a beautiful Sunday morning. The rhythm of my gait brings me to a tiny park, which appears to have once blended with the clean sidewalks of the Alameda. Over time, however, the park's luster has given way to the dust of the tracks. The trampled grass is now beige, the lone slide in the center of the park banged and bruised. A few abandoned picnic tables remain, missing the families sharing tostadas around them. Along the park's peripheral path, *federales* pace. These agents don hefty black boots laced to the tops of their shins. Their bulky jackets match the black boots, and each man has a Mexican flag embroidered on his shoulder. Helmets shield their faces, their heads resembling turtles under immense shells. But what most catches the eye are the massive machine guns slung over their shoulders. These are the agents who "reprimand" migrants—meaning anything from ignoring, helping, arresting, deporting, assaulting, robbing, raping or threatening.

As I continue my jog around a park most people would not choose to run in, I think back to my recent conversation with Jesús Magaña Villaseñor, an employee at the Guanajuato State Institute for Attention toward Guanajuato Migrants and their Families. During the interview, I had gingerly prodded the subject of Central American migration through Guanajuato. Jesús distanced the Institute from this quagmire, maintaining that the organization focused on the rights of Mexican migrants and that Central Americans did not fall under their purview. I pushed back cautiously. "But if Central Americans are passing through Guanajuato every day, isn't it the state's issue?"

"Yes," he answered. "Yes, it should be the state's issue, and the federal government's issue, but each state has its institutions that are directed to support a particular topic. In this case, our purpose is to help *guanajuatenses* and their families." Jesús later admitted that perhaps the Institute and the state could do a better job of directing Central Americans to their counties' consulates to report abuses, though he still emphasized that these immigrants were not the Institute's—or the state's—prerogative.

I pause from my run to stretch and observe the *federales*. Perhaps these "human rights" institutes are not so concerned about Central

Americans, but those intimidating men in black certainly are. With the government so focused on "reprimanding" migrants, is there anyone left to protect their rights? What happens, I wonder, when the government is focused on "reprimanding" migrants, yet no one is dedicated to protecting their rights? Obviously, those rights will be trampled upon. Hence, the stories of robbery and assault on the part of migrant officers that roll through the shelter every week.

I leave the barren border park and reenter the tidy sidewalks of the Alameda. Here, a lazy Sunday morning stretches indefinitely; here, the dust of the train tracks never settles.

"Okay, the doors are closing for the night. No one else can leave and no one can come," Lupita declared as she slammed the shelter's black iron door. It was one of my first sessions at the migrant shelter in September 2016, and locking everyone in at 7:00 PM felt odd. Yet it was also a reminder of another hazard that migrants face. In this case, *federales* were patrolling right outside the shelter, ready to arrest and detain any person with Central American features that ventured in or out. For those inside the shelter, the threat of deportation loomed from the moment they crossed the Mexico-Guatemalan border.

As Lupita bolted the door with authority, I asked the group next to me about the immigration patrol in Celaya. One man let out a chortle. "*Por todos lados está mal,*" he explained, shaking his head. Everywhere it's bad. "Here is no different." He went on to explain that only two departments of the Mexican government could legally deal with policing undocumented Central Americans: the Instituto Nacional de Migración (INM) and the federal police force (*federales*), (although in certain areas the military, and more recently, the National Guard, have also gotten involved). However, because the INM is not technically a law enforcement body, they charge armed *federales* with patrolling areas frequented by migrants, including Celaya's migrant shelter. Apparently, *federales* began scouring the migrant shelter entrance from 6:00 PM onward every night, knowing that many migrants would be arriving late in the evening and would seek refuge in the shelter. I pictured the men who roamed just beyond the iron barricade of the shelter, their machine guns clutched high across their chests. In many ways, it was a bizarre game of tag—complete with the taggers "puppy guarding" the home base, waiting for their targets to come out. Except this system was rooted in the law, turning actual life questions—such as one's safety or the right to seek out a better life—into a game.

While the *federales* played cat-and-mouse with the Central Americans, Mexico's leadership tried to maintain a precarious dual stance on immigration. On one hand, then-President Enrique Peña Nieto portrayed himself as a protector of migrants' human rights, willing to stand up to the xenophobia espoused by then presidential candidate Donald Trump. At the September 19, 2016 convention of the United Nations Summit for Refugees and Migrants, Peña Nieto gave a speech emphasizing that Mexico had consistently been a nation of "origin, transit, destination, and return for people," and would continue to be so even if Trump was elected.[1] Despite this rhetoric, Trump and Peña Nieto agreed on one thing: deporting Central American migrants before they reached the US should be a priority for Mexico.

Indeed, before Trump even ran for office, Peña Nieto had already launched initiatives to increase immigration vigilance throughout Mexico. In response to the 2014 influx of unaccompanied Central American minors to the U.S, Mexico implemented "Plan Frontera Sur," which amplified the nation's immigration patrol at twelve key points of entry along the border with Guatemala and Belize. As a result, arrests of Central American migrants in Mexico increased from 78,000 in 2013 to 170,000 in 2014.[2] That's a jump of nearly one hundred thousand apprehensions in just one year. Clearly, Mexico was no longer a place of "transit" or "destination."

Support from the Obama Administration played a significant role in Plan Frontera Sur, both by diplomatically pressuring the Peña Nieto administration to plug the porous border, and by allocating funds to the Instituto Nacional de Migración. In 2016 alone, the US gave $75 million to the INM, which was in charge of carrying out Plan Frontera Sur.[3] In this sense, the Obama administration was also trying to maintain a double standard: championing pro-immigrant discourse at home, while simultaneously arranging for the deportation of thousands of unaccompanied minors before they ever became a problem for the United States.

Since the launch of Plan Frontera Sur, the US government has continually pressed Mexico to adopt migration policy rooted in national security, similar to the immigration ethos of the United States. However, in a country like Mexico, where corruption runs rampant and human rights violations are commonplace, treating migrants as a national security threat only further dehumanizes them. As the Instituto para la Seguridad y la Democracia (Insyde), states in a comprehensive analysis of Mexico's INM, "The adoption of a migration policy that is connected to or subsumed in the national security policy, has also produced excesses in the use of authority by migration agents, excesses in the powers and the use of force by local and federal police as well as a tendency toward opacity in the Institute's management and performance."[4] In other words, if migrants are treated as security threat, their human rights can evaporate.

President Trump, in his typical confrontational style, has personally amped up the pressure on Mexico to quell Central American migration. Over the first half of 2019, for instance, Trump repeatedly threatened to shut down the entire US–Mexican border if Mexico's subsequent president, Andres Manuel López Obrador, did not immediately halt illegal immigration. In the fall of 2018, Trump painted the caravans advancing toward the border as a grave security threat and insisted that Mexico stop them. Once he took office in December, López Obrador largely declined to get into a battle of words with Trump; instead, he attempted to balance the coercion from the north with trying to better protect migrant rights, which had been one of his campaign promises. On March 28, 2019, just a day before Trump tweeted about closing the border, López Obrador remarked, "We are going to do everything we can to help. We don't in any way want a confrontation with the US government."[5]

Despite Trump's warnings, López Obrador largely accommodated several caravans that traveled through Mexico after he first took office on December 1, 2018, creating a legal path to transit through the country by fast tracking one-year humanitarian visas. However, the program ended in February 2019 after about 13,000 visas were issued.[6] Since then, the administration has been slower in awarding overall humanitarian visas, claiming it is prioritizing them for the most "vulnerable" populations.

While reducing access to humanitarian visas, López Obrador has continued Peña Nieto's policy of deporting thousands of migrants. Although the number of people deported from Mexico in the first three months of López Obrador's presidency dropped 17 percent compared to the same period the previous year, the summer months brought a significant rise in deportations.[7] Between January and August

2019, Mexico deported approximately 102,314 Central Americans to Guatemala, a 63 percent increase from Peña Nieto's administration over the first six months of 2018.[8] This sharp rise corresponded to the threatened tariffs and increased pressure from the Trump administration. Ultimately, by summer 2019, López Obrador could no longer afford to ignore Trump's threats, acceding to the fervent anti-immigration rhetoric-turned-policy emblematic of the US president. With the National Guard and the military more involved in policing migrants, it remains to be seen how the crackdown on Central Americans in Mexico will evolve.

The New Trump Paradigm in Mexico

It was an absurdly hot fall day in Celaya, and I was doing my typical Friday afternoon activity—sitting on a bench in the plaza people watching as pigeons frolicked in the fountains. It was not unusual for someone to notice me on these occasions, take a seat on the bench, and ask where I was from. (After all, I stood out!) On this Friday, the woman who plopped herself beside me was a rounded *señora*, her peg-like legs sticking straight out as she maneuvered her bottom toward the back of the bench. Her hair was dyed red and segregated into easy-to-maintain grandma curls. We quickly covered the basics: where I was from, how I'd ended up in Celaya, what local attractions I'd seen (out of the three), and if I liked the food. When I began to talk about my work at the shelter, however, this well-mannered grandma went off on an impassioned monologue.

"Those migrants they come here, they never leave," she began, her tiny legs stretching toward the ground. "Supposedly they're going to the United States, but then they just stay here instead and cause problems for our country." She proceeded to go off on the "they take our jobs" and "they commit crimes" narratives that were all too familiar to me. For fifteen minutes she ranted, her hand gestures intensifying wildly as she grew ever more animated. Her arguments were based on stereotypes and fears rather than any hard evidence. And yes, she had a son in Los Angeles.

While the majority of Mexicans I spoke with were vehemently anti-Trump and pro-immigration reform, a small number were also concerned, like this woman, about Central American "infiltrators" remaining in Mexico. Those people are different, they would say. They aren't *us*. According to a 2008 case study done by the Instituto para la Seguridad y la Democracia in Tapachula (a southern border town in the state of Chiapas), "60 percent of the population did not feel migration offered benefits; of these respondents, 36 percent believed that migrants committed crimes, 30 percent thought they encouraged gang activity, 17 percent considered them to have a corrupting influence on society, and 6 percent thought they destroyed homes."[9] While such perceptions may be more pronounced in a border state like Chiapas, they did not materially differ from public sentiment in Celaya. Certainly, there were those who spoke of supporting Central American arrivals—and took direct measures to do so—but the general public seemed less inclined.

As public opinion decries the influx of Central Americans, the Mexican government typically follows, advancing oppositional international and domestic stances. As the executive director of Insyde, Ernesto López Portillo, puts it: "The balance is absurd: Mexico does not offer migrants what it demands from others for its own migrants."[10] In the age of Donald Trump, this paradox is more pronounced than ever.

On another sweltering afternoon, I witnessed first-hand the early impacts of the Trump phenomenon. The day before, frustrated in my efforts to interview government officials, I had been sent away from the state's Institute for Migrant Attention office. This time, however, the office manager invited me to a conference on migration, where two congressmen and other "important people" would be speaking. "I'll introduce you to them," he offered. I accepted the invitation, grateful for his welcome (but seemingly random) attitude shift.

We gathered in a stuffy auditorium at Querétaro's university. The event certainly looked important, as women in impossibly high heels and shoulder-padded jackets greeted middle-aged men with meticulously groomed mustaches. They all smiled at the right moments and knew exactly when to ease into a new circle to network. It was not all that different from the elite world of politics in the United States.

Beyond my obvious foreigner status, there were other ways that I didn't fit in. There were codes I hadn't practiced, rehearsed etiquettes that seemed clunky when I tried them out. To make matters worse, I couldn't recognize my contact from the migration office. Did he have a beard? Was his hair starting to gray? Middle-aged? Or older? My brain kept convincing me that each man over thirty in the crowd was him. "I'm 80 percent sure that's him," my sister (who was visiting at the time) asserted, gesturing to a man hunched over his cellphone in the front row.

I left my "professional" (more school grade) bag with my sister and casually strolled to the front row, trying to maintain a delicate balance between looking like I was going to approach this man and appearing to simply roam around.

"Buenos días," I nodded when passing him. I felt satisfied with the cool way the words flowed from my mouth. Except he didn't look up from his cellphone. "Buenos días," I offered again, as any chance of being graceful rapidly disintegrated. As he glanced upward, I searched his eyes for any trace of recognition. Nothing.

"Buenos días," he finally responded politely, a thread of confusion wound up in his voice. Definitely not him. I sauntered onward.

"I'm not 80 percent sure anymore," my sister whispered to me as I slouched back into my seat.

The event started an hour and a half late, as many of the legislators were stuck in traffic from Mexico City. From the conference description, I had assumed the discussion would be about Central American migration to Mexico. No such luck. Once again, that was a topic no one seemed to want to broach. Instead, the politicians diverted to talking about Trump and the millions of Mexicans up north who could potentially face deportation.

"What has changed with Trump is not so much the number of people being deported, as who is being deported," began Dr. Eunice Rendón Cárdenas, the former director of Mexico's Institute for Mexicans Abroad. (At that point, that assertion was true, as Trump had not yet begun his threatened mass deportations.) Cárdenas spoke quickly, her hand gestures barely keeping up with her words. With Trump, she emphasized, Mexico was seeing a completely new profile of deportees. Through the American administration's executive order on deportation, the priority for border control had shifted from deporting those who had committed "serious crimes" (as it was under Obama) to removing anyone who had committed any sort of crime. For Mexico, this would mean an increase in deportees who had spent most of their lives in the States, who barely knew their "home" country of Mexico, including more Dreamer youth. How would Mexico support these returnees (who may not even speak Spanish) in their transition?

Cárdenas seemed like the type of go-getter who wanted more out of her (largely corrupt) government. There should be more support for returners, she contended. There should be government-funded psychologists to help deportees through the emotions of the transition, especially for those leaving family across the border. There should be a mentorship program between recent deportees and those who had returned previously. There should be a new program where returnees can receive a certification for skills they learned up north, like English. There should be more efforts to connect returnees with potential employers. There was passion and thoughtfulness behind the ideas she articulated, and it gave me hope.

At the same time, however, it was difficult to imagine the actual implementation of these programs, especially as the Mexican government's response to the issue of returnees seemed to be more about generating positive publicity than actually helping people. For example, one of the government's "solutions" to addressing the challenges of returnees, a program known as "*Bienvenido a casa paisano*," (translated to "Welcome Home Countrymen") is based around informational modules located in various outposts in each state. The module in Querétaro was stationed at the bus terminal. Returnees could come to these modules and receive a pamphlet containing "useful" information such as how much cash you can bring into Mexico, or how to register your car. Perhaps these details benefit select Mexicans, but they seem extraneous for most, whose fundamental concerns are more about where to live and how to support themselves.

Moreover, the modules are only in-service during holiday periods, i.e. Christmas, Semana Santa, and summer vacation. Two days after Semana Santa, I spent a day trying to track down the module in Querétaro, only to find that it was gone. Why would the government only staff the modules during holidays? Because the program was geared toward well-off Mexicans coming home for the holidays—not recent deportees needing assistance. Plus, Mexico's bus stations would be teeming with people heading on vacation, who might nod approvingly at the module and say, "Look at all the government is doing to help." It is all about the veneer of aiding, not truly supporting returnees.

Back at the conference, an audience member was the first to mention Central American migrants. What could the federal government do about the Central Americans deported from up north and dropped on the Mexican side of the border? How did officials support these deportees? The speakers instead focused on how Mexico could pressure Washington into taking them back. Dr. Jorge Castañeda Gutman, the former Secretary of International Relations, asserted, "We have no governmental presence along the US–Mexican border," which he claimed allowed for these populations of deported Central Americans to be left in Mexico. Although in Gutman's words, "The INM is one of the most corrupt institutes in Mexico," he still argued that if it were better represented at the border, the Border Patrol would have to prove an individual was Mexican before dumping them on the other side. This would be a way to tip the scales back in Mexico's favor. The panelists of course had no idea that Mexico would soon be bullied into housing thousands more Central Americans along the border as they awaited their US asylum cases. Mexico's leverage—with or without a strong INM presence along the border—was minimal.

In four hours of discussion, not once did any of the representatives substantially speak about Central Americans migrants transiting through Mexico. Even when a graduate student explicitly asked how the federal government could better protect these individuals against kidnapping, assault, and rape, each speaker deflected and digressed. There were no good answers. If they broke the surface of that quagmire, they would have to confront the corruption that lay beneath.

A panel of Mexican government officials take questions during the forum on migration, Universidad Autónoma de Querétaro.

The Instituto Nacional de Migración

The stories were endless. *That officer by the train robbed me. That one pulled me off the train and beat me. That one threatened to kill me if I didn't give him everything I had.* In almost every group of migrants I spoke with, at least one had been robbed or assaulted by a Mexican migration officer. Often there were several. "When *la migra* grabs you," one migrant noted, "you can't fight back like with other criminals. You just better hope you've got what they're looking for."

"*La migra*" in Mexico is comprised of two government entities that are authorized to patrol for and arrest undocumented migrants: the federal police (federales) and the Instituto Nacional de Migración (INM). Corruption has corroded many of Mexico's governmental agencies, but the INM may be one of the worst. According to a report by the Institute for Security and Democracy (INSYDE), a Mexican civil society organization, a number of structural factors contribute to the INM's capacity for degeneracy, including low salaries, inexperienced and undertrained officers, deficient controls, and ineffective sanctions for abuses.[11] These issues—combined with migrants' lack of resources—are a recipe for corruption throughout the organization.

The INM is a diffuse agency with a significant amount of autonomy, leaving little oversight of the organization. Created in 1993 and designated as a national security organization in 2005, the INM is run by a president-appointed commissioner who manages procedures from Mexico City. Under the commissioner, there are thirty-two delegates in each of Mexico's states who control regional affairs. The actual officers, however, work in the most remote corners of each state, making it difficult for even delegates to know their daily operations. Furthermore, the delegates are not required to report officers' actions to any kind of regional headquarters, so there is almost no incentive for them to track what their officers are doing, much less discipline them. Geographically dispersed positions and a lack of oversight mean that officers face little accountability.

Politically motivated hiring practices and lack of training also mean that officers, midlevel positions, and senior managers are not properly prepared to do their jobs. The INM infrequently posts new positions, and instead seems to hire officer, mid-level and senior positions based on party and family ties.[12] Hiring under-qualified individuals not only compromises the functionality of the organization, but it also brings in employees who may have no commitment to migrant rights, or knowledge of the issues at stake.

The lack of training for new or potential INM employees also contributes to an atmosphere of disorder. Although new employees are nominally trained, no training academy occurs prior to hiring, which would weed out ill-suited candidates. Additionally, the training that does exist does not include an exam, leaving participants with no means of demonstrating their capability to apply this training. According to INSYDE, training in the INM is an exercise in "checking the boxes."[13] The goal is certainly not to cultivate a culture of human rights within the Institute. With little experience, minimal training, and no oversight, new officers are thrown out into the field with full autonomy—for better or worse.

The Institute's salary structure also does not incentivize good behavior. As INSYDE notes, there are major pay discrepancies between positions: "Whereas an Area Director receives a net monthly salary of at least MX $31,693.80 and a Director General receives a net monthly salary of at least MX$73,833.94, a "B" Class Federal Migration Agent receives a mere MX$7,372.05 as a net monthly salary."[14] (For reference, I was paid MX$12,000 per month as an English teaching assistant.) Thus, the most dangerous jobs and the positions that deal directly with migrants (officers) are paid the least. While low salaries do not necessarily engender corruption and high salaries certainly don't always prevent it, a low salary—combined with minimal room for advancement within the INM—means that there is little incentive to excel at the job.[15]

While not incentivizing good behavior, the Institute simultaneously does not reprimand misdeeds. Internally, there are two oversight offices: The Officer of Internal Oversight (OIC) and the Internal Affairs Unit, which fall under the Secretariat of the Interior (the agency that manages the INM).[16] While the OIC is designed to receive and deal with complaints, it has very limited personnel, all of whom work in Mexico City. Additionally, the OIC only conducts an investigation if it receives notice of a violation from another agency. They do not conduct proactive investigations. Because the OIC does not seek out such complaints, the system relies on departments within the INM and other agencies to actively report abuses, which almost never occurs.

The second oversight office, the Internal Affairs Unit, was created in 2013 but is still getting off the ground. It remains to be seen whether it will have any kind of impact. Migrants that have the gumption to report INM abuses can use complaint boxes in some INM offices. However, because there are so few offices, it requires extraordinary effort just to turn in a complaint, especially without any hope of receiving a response.

For the very few abuses that are reported, the current system of sanctions is hugely inadequate. In theory, any report of misconduct should spur an investigation, with the potential for employment and legal consequences. In practice, however, either nothing happens, or—if the report is deemed serious enough—the officer is either fired or laterally transferred to another position. As the INSYDE report notes, the INM prefers to have officers resign or transfer rather than fire them in order to avoid labor disputes with the union and severance pay.[17] If an officer is transferred, nothing prevents them from continuing to work in the INM and commit the same abuses.

As if the lack of oversight and consequences for misconduct were not enough, the INM also has no policy governing the use of force for its agents. Technically, INM agents are not allowed to carry guns. Instead, *federales* are contracted to provide armed security to the INM whenever they formally request it.[18] Because officers are unarmed, the INM maintains that this policy alone protects against the misuse of force. However, there are plenty of ways to exert force without a gun.

Physical beatings, welding a club, robbery, and simply threatening using one's power as an INM officer are commonplace. Without a specific policy outlining these practices as misconduct, there is unlikely to be consequences for those who utilize them.

While there are two more humanitarian wings of the INM, both face the same lack of oversight and accountability. The first sub agency, known as Grupo Beta, does search and rescue operations, receives complaints, and provides humanitarian assistance and legal advice. However, the group is minimally funded, and has few personnel, with only twenty-two units operating in nine states across Mexico. Additionally, when Grupo Beta agents receive complaints, there is no standardized process for reporting abuses. According to the Washington Office on Latin America, there have been many inconsistencies with Grupo Beta reports, with some containing significant detail, others minimal, and many submitted to authorities who have no power to investigate.[19] And since Grupo Beta falls under the INM, if their agents receive complaints about INM officers or *federales*, they are hesitant to pass them on for fear of retribution.

The second wing, the Child Protection Officers (OPIs), generally have a background in social services and work specifically with unaccompanied minors. The same structural deficiencies also apply to OPIs, combined with very little training. For both groups, and the INM in general, organized crime also impedes their work. When criminal networks weld more power than the government, instances of collusion dominate. Even if the oversight, accountability, and incentives were well-designed in the Instituto Nacional de Migración, it still would be very difficult to run a non-corrupt agency in a country where cartels have the last word.

While the Mexican government has drastically expanded its

capacity to detain and deport Central Americans, especially with coercion from President Trump, it still refuses to concentrate on the crimes perpetuated against them, especially when committed by state officials. This trend is unlikely to change anytime soon. As a young man told me one time at the shelter, "We always have to prove that we are human, not just migrants."

PART FOUR

BECAUSE POWER MATTERS

Ten

GENDER, WHITENESS, AND PRIVILEGE

The author accompanies Rosaura as she searches for work in Celaya, in an effort to mitigate her vulnerability as a migrant woman alone.

TWO WEEKS INTO MY TIME in Celaya, and I still couldn't direct my coworker to my house. "I think it's left," I offered from the passenger seat as we circled the block yet again. "There it is!" I pointed ahead to a dilapidated sign, the only marker of my home.

"*Este barrio está feo,*" my coworker blurted out as he slowed to drop me off. The English translation indicated that I lived in either a bad neighborhood or an ugly one. I didn't bother asking him for a clarification, however, as it didn't matter either way—my neighborhood was both bad and ugly.

"It may be ugly, but it suits me," I responded, the words slipping out, but their meaning uncertain to me. Did this place actually suit me? Everything on the street was visibly run-down. The sidewalk was marred by decades' worth of scars: a labyrinth of cracks that fractured out into the street; divots and holes and randomly scattered bricks; flattened trash that had been repeatedly run over; the occasional stray dog taking a nap in the gutter. At the corner, the sidewalk abruptly ended in a pile of bricks, the remnants of an unfinished wall that extended into the street.

Like many residential streets in Mexico, you couldn't really see the houses, as each structure was nestled behind a gate, wall, or some sort of iron slab. Thus, it was impossible to tell if the house behind the barricade was immaculate and took up the whole block, or if there was nothing back there but rubble. My house was somewhere on the modest side of in-between. The front was made up of a cream-colored metal wall with a sign outside reading "Doctor Felipe González" (not sure why—there was no doctor's office). The peeling paint at the bottom of the wall was slowly creeping upward, as was the case with almost all of the houses on the block—except for one, which had a nicely painted peach wall with a tree neatly pruned into a spiral out front. It looked slightly out of place next to the decaying gray apartments with the barred windows next door.

During those first few weeks in Celaya, I was reading Joan Didion's *Slouching Towards Bethlehem*. In the book's prologue, Didion references the common themes that run through her stories: disorder, chaos, things coming apart from the center. As I read further, I found that my neighborhood began to fit these descriptions, as there was a kind of illogical order that governed everything. Conventional beauty may not have been its attraction, but there was something comforting, even beautiful—like a Didion story—about living on a street that didn't prune the disorder out of its trees. There was beauty in the woman who spent her days sitting outside her corner store, her pudgy legs sprawled out over the edge of the sidewalk, always ready with a genuine greeting. There was beauty in the house a few doors down that left its doors open so that the chickens could roam freely into the street. And there was beauty in the old man who always seemed to be asleep in his chair, his chin folded into his collar. The street didn't subscribe to a homogenous idea of niceness; it was its own world of people and things in motion, an oxymoronic blend of chaotic synchronicity.

If I could find beauty in my conventionally ugly neighborhood, I came to believe that there must also be some sort of beauty in all of the conventionally unpleasant emotions I had experienced since arriving in Celaya—loneliness, restlessness, the unshakable sense that I just didn't belong. Despite these feelings, there was something pro-foundly authentic—maybe even beautiful—about being able to sit with my silent observations as I strolled around the city, taking note of the palm tree that was silhouetted against the last fragments of the day, its strands of hair dripping downward; the grandfather and grandson riding their horses down a busy street with their sombreros stretch-ing over their shoulders like umbrellas; the stained glass windows of a nearby church that cast blue, red, and yellow beams over the space in front of me. To sit with just my thoughts on a bus to Guadalajara. To sit with my loneliness as I ate ice cream in bed by myself. And to live with my emptiness as I yearned for family, friends, and those daily remind-ers that I was loved. It wasn't the opposite of happiness, but maybe just a more layered form of it—the kind that was mixed with sadness and solitude and a potent longing to feel at home in this new, ugly, yet beautiful, place that somehow suited me.

Rosaura

As I tried to get used to my new surroundings in Mexico, I began to meet others who were going through the same adjustment—in particular, Central Americans passing through a country that was decidedly different from their own. Although the goal of these migrants was to reach the US, many were stalled on their journey, forced to stop and earn money before continuing onward. In their interlude in Mexico, these Hondurans, Guatemalans, and Salvadorians had to learn the many facets of a new country. The language may have been the same, but the words people used were certainly not. The weather may have still been hot, but the *clima* varied markedly. The cultural cues, the

Rosaura, maintaining hope at El Refugio.

emphasis on family, may have felt like home, but their families were not there. While I could relate to some of these fundamental feelings of culture shock, there were key aspects of their experiences I would never know—namely, the feeling of being undocumented in Mexico, of being considered a second-class citizen.

Soon after meeting Rosaura, a single Guatemalan woman in her mid-fifties, we embarked on a bus excursion downtown. She teetered on the curb as we waited for the bus, which could come anytime in the next two to fifty minutes. One bus zoomed by so quickly that I barely had time to read the handwritten placard on the windshield that told travelers where it was headed.

"*¿Es nuestro camión?*" Rosaura asked, the big blue bus already past us.

"No, we're waiting for the yellow one that says '*centro*,'" I replied, momentarily forgetting that Rosaura could not read well enough to know which bus to take.

Rosaura approaches every vendor in Celaya's mercado to inquire about work.

Our destination was the *mercado* downtown, where Rosaura and I would go from booth to booth, asking if this flower stand, or that fruit vendor, needed help. Like many migrants, Rosaura was in limbo, as she had to find work in Celaya if she had any hope of continuing *al norte.* In addition to getting her down to the market, my job was to make sure no one took advantage of her. As a single woman with no papers, it wasn't safe for her to look for work by herself, as she could be kidnapped, raped, or sucked into a dangerous job. Power dynamics being what they were, our levels of vulnerability as women were not the same.

Rosaura knew all too well the consequences of being optionless in Mexico. When I first met her at Celaya's long-term migrant shelter, she sat alone at the edge of a table, flipping dominoes absentmindedly as she gazed downward. As we began to talk, she seemed both withdrawn in her own world and delightfully social. Her genuine interest showed in her steady gaze as she asked me what I was doing in Celaya. She soaked in my story like a supportive mom, asking questions in all the right places. Two small ringlets of gray-streaked hair bordered her forehead and her black curly hair was groomed back into a tight ponytail. She leaned in warmly as she spoke.

When it was her turn to share, she told me that was waiting for any sign of her husband, who had vanished a month before. She wistfully recalled his disappearance. "We arrived (in Celaya) on a Monday, the two of us," she began with conviction, clearly intent on recounting her story in detail. "In the afternoon, we arrived tired because the bus left us at the station and we walked all the way here. We got here. They gave us food. In the morning we woke up, we bathed, we ate breakfast." She emphasized the normalcy of the day, hanging on to these everyday moments when she had no idea that they would be the last times she ate with, slept by, or saw her husband of ten years.

She continued. "Then he said to me, 'let's go ask for money . . .' So there we went, looking for work too, asking around to see if there was some job. And a man told my husband that he should meet him at a place six blocks from there. He told him, 'come in the afternoon, and they'll give you an answer about a job.' So (my husband) told me, 'you stay at the migrant shelter and I'll go.'" Rosaura's bright eyes shrunk as she glanced up. "But he never came back, never, never." Her voice faded as she receded into a cast of gloom.

Rosaura then began to speculate on what might have happened to him. I imagined that she spent much of her empty time at the shelter doing so. "It could be that they caught him or that he just left, I don't know, I don't know, I haven't heard from him." Her brain seemed to be looping around in a familiar circle. "I don't know, I don't know, I haven't heard from him. He hasn't even spoken to his family in Guatemala, no. His mom doesn't know where he is either. No. She doesn't know." Rosaura had dissected every possible explanation, as had her mother-in-law. "His mom asks me, 'Why don't you know what happened if you were traveling together? You don't know anything?' But I tell her, I don't know anything. I mean sometimes we fought, like any couple, but it wasn't enough for him to just leave." I could see an unwritten question mark hanging in her voice—there was just no way to know what had happened, no way to settle a mind that was searching for answers.

Rosaura did report her missing husband to the police and to the Red Cross in charge of the shelter, despite her status as an undocumented Guatemalan in Mexico. But she was not optimistic that they would find him. She noted how unidentifiable bodies turned up all the time, referencing the case of three recently discovered corpses in nearby Irapuato that were too rotted to identify.

This was not the first time Rosaura and her husband had

attempted the journey north. In 2015, the couple had traveled by freight train through Mexico, only to be detained at the border and deported back to Guatemala City, their city of origin. During the two years that Rosaura was back in the city, she felt increasingly fearful for her life. Violence worsened in the capital as organized crime commanded the streets, and her family was not rich enough to be afforded immunity.

"My brother also disappeared there," Rosaura shared as she thought back on the last few years. Her husband's disappearance was thus not Rosaura's first experience with this terrible waiting and wondering game. "My brother disappeared with his wife and his three kids, and we don't know what happened. This happened like four, six months ago. We don't know what happened." Rosaura's brother had had a business in Guatemala City, and gangs began to demand an increasing portion of his earnings. When he couldn't pay their quota, he and his entire family disappeared. He didn't take the threats seriously, Rosaura said, and then one day the whole family was gone.

Uneasiness coursed through my veins. How could it be that ordinary people just vanished without a trace? How could this warm woman have had so many people ripped suddenly from her life? I imagined that with tragedy so commonplace, the ability to feel safe was irretrievably lost, replaced by gnawing, ungrounded fear and uncertainty.

Soon after her brother disappeared, Rosaura and her husband began to receive threats. Unable to ignore the harassment, the couple decided upon another journey across borders. Rosaura's niece had arrived in Texas a few months earlier, after gangs murdered her husband. Again, it was for the same reason—the gang had blacklisted the man for being unable to pay the extortion fees they demanded. "She just can't go back to her country," Rosaura reflected. It became increasingly clear that the same was true for Rosaura.

"Did you consider applying for political asylum?" I asked. She shook her head. Like Fernando, Rosaura had no faith in the legal system. "No, I didn't ask for asylum because they detain you for more time. Sometimes, yes, they give it to you, and sometimes not." In a backlogged system, Rosaura also knew that the process could take years— time likely spent in an immigration jail cell. Better to risk the journey and undocumented life in the States than hand someone the keys to her potential deportation.

The other reason Rosaura had left her country was poverty, which exacerbated her vulnerability to the pervasive violence around her. "I don't have anywhere to live," she said, a stark summary of her life in Guatemala City. She would stay with her adult children, but she had no job or way to support herself. "I went around taking things out of the trash." Like so many in transit, she was simply seeking a job and the sense of security that goes with it.

She described that now, halfway to the border, she would daydream about being in America. "What do those dreams look like?" I inquired. They were not filled with material goods, she answered. Rather, they were about working.

"I'd imagine myself working, working, having a job . . . and helping my family because they have so little . . . Well it was my dream to support my family . . ." Her voice softened as she wondered if this dream would ever become reality. With her husband missing, her family now consisted of her two children in their twenties and her mother, all of whom still lived in Guatemala City. Rosaura emphasized she would take any job to help support them. Having left, she expressed fear that something horrendous might happen to them. Too much had already transpired for me to assuage her worries.

"I was trying to go to Houston to reach these dreams." She laughed nervously, making light of her volatile circumstances. "But I couldn't make it." She paused, as if trying to decide whether that was the end of her story.

Not only was Rosaura dealing with the grief of losing her husband and her brother and his family, but she was also trying to figure out her next move. "I'm a little afraid to keep going alone, if there's no help from family." Rosaura knew the dangers of the trip north and was aware that as a woman traveling alone, there was a good chance that she could be raped. Without her husband's support (or even just his presence), she was infinitely more vulnerable. Given the gang threats that had driven her out of Guatemala City, going home wasn't an option either. So, Rosaura had stayed in the migrant shelter in Celaya for the past month, looking for work and praying for signs of her husband.

Her constant job search had so far brought nothing. "Not just any-one is going to give you a job without papers," she decried. Indeed, the demand for unskilled undocumented labor in Mexico was nowhere near that of the US. "If I find a job, well I'll stay here, and if not, well maybe they'll deport me. I still don't know. I've already spent so much time here." Voicing these words seemed to dissipate her hope like a deflating balloon. There was no good choice. She was stuck in the middle of a draining journey with nothing left to do but wait.

"How does the waiting affect you?" I asked, knowing full well the answer.

"Ahhhh," she began, tears already rolling to the brim of her eyelids. "It affects me a lot." The words came out in a whisper, the weight of her emotions dampening their volume. She pursed her lips, clearly trying not to cry, to no avail. Undulating ripples of anguish creased her forehead as her eyebrows squished in toward her nose. Between her tears, she added, "Because I'm so far from family . . . And this city is difficult and dangerous as a woman. So many things that happen."

Her face showed many layers of tortured emotion. The wonder-

With no leads on work, Rosaura heads back to *El Refugio*.

ing about and grieving for her husband. The longing for her family at home. The swelling weight of the journey behind her. The heavy question of what to do next. And on top of all that was the enormity of being a woman alone in a foreign land. I had felt that at times in Celaya as well. Those moments when I would walk home under the sinking sun, my pace quickening as stories of recent murders echoed in my mind. Or when the alcoholic neighbor banged on my door looking for booze, and I would hide until he finally left. Or when the mechanics by my house would shout vulgarities while I waited at the bus stop, and I'd grip the mace in my purse. As a woman, you try not to wear your vulnerability on your sleeve, but it tends to leak out regardless.

Rosaura and I may have shared some degree of gender vulnerability in Celaya, but she bore burdens I never would. She lamented that there seemed to be nothing she could do to mitigate her exposure. "At least I'm in a wholesome place," she recognized, looking around her as three little kids kicked a ball around on the patio. She smiled at the scene. "Walking helps me clear my mind," she added. "And when one occupies their mind in work, the sadness and the worry goes away. Being here with nothing to do makes one think more."

Existing inside the walls of the shelter was both a blessing and a curse for Rosaura. She had a place to wait. She played with the children at the shelter. But grief and vulnerability—those two ugly snakes—still choked away her brightness.

La Madrina

There was something about the whole experience that left me feeling suffocated . . . with friendliness. I had been in Celaya for three days and was already overwhelmed by well-wishers—coworkers translating every Spanish word, my temporary host family feeding me endlessly, a new friend calling me every few minutes to make sure I was okay. Transitioning to a relational culture from an individualistic society was proving to be an adjustment.

One day a coworker named Luis offered to show me around downtown. So there I was, on my own personal tour of a new city, and all I wanted was to find my way back home and go to bed. I needed some space. But the evening was not about to end anytime soon. I found myself at yet another restaurant (because I *must* be hungry), talking to Luis about his favorite places in Guanajuato. I mention that I'd like to see Querétaro. We'll go Saturday, he replies. I tell him that

I like to go running. He makes a date for us to run on Sunday at a local park. I ask him about a nearby hot spring. He plans to take me to some cabins there the following weekend. Blatant references to my boyfriend in the US don't seem to slow Luis down. He is intent on showing me every last corner of Guanajuato.

I casually tell him that I am looking for a room to rent for my nine-month stay. Of course, his godmother has an extra one. But before I can see the room, it's *la hija de la madrina's* birthday today, and we cannot show up to the house without a cake. And to get the right cake we *have* to take a bus to the other side of downtown. An hour later, we are in *la madrina's* living room, a heaping pile of cake on my plate, surrounded by Luis's entire family. After kissing the checks of all seventeen of his relatives, I stuff every bite of cake into my already full belly with a smile, wondering why this family I don't know has invited me to this birthday party.

A few hours later, once the celebration has finally fizzled out, *la madrina* takes me aside to show me the rest of the house. The grand finale to the evening. She is the *abuela* type—short, rounded, with curly dyed hair. Her shrill voice alternates between nagging and soothing. "*Cuidadito con las escaleritas. Son pequeñitas, mi hijita,*" she squeaks, taking me by the arm. "Be a little careful with the little stairs. They're teeny tiny, my little girl." She repeats the warning several times. I am not a religious person, but I would have to find Jesus if I lived in this house. He is everywhere: crucified in the hallways, standing in every bedroom, posing in portraits on every wall.

On cue, *La madrina* inquires about my religion. "*Eres católica, ¿no?*"

"Well, my mom was Catholic and my dad is Jewish, so *yo soy una mezcla,*" I respond, trying to preserve the hope in her eyes that I am indeed a moral person.

"Well," she says. "We pray twice a day, so you'll pray with us." Her enthusiasm is both endearing and disconcerting.

We step out onto the patio. Her little Chihuahua leaps toward me; as far as I can tell, this dog's sole purpose in life is to yap and poop. I tip-toe between the poop pellets littering the floor as *la madrina* escorts me around the rest of the house.

Before I leave, *la madrina* hugs me one last time. She wraps my hands in her rough palms, looks me in the eye, and says, "You are a beautiful person."

"*Igualmente*," I answer. "So are you."

"And, of course I wouldn't charge you to stay here," she adds. "I too have a daughter who doesn't live at home, so I know what it's like to be a worried mother. Oh, your mother must be so worried! I'll take care of you!" I picture my mother sitting in her kitchen thousands of miles away. No doubt, she is worried about me. She would be grateful to know that *la madrina* and everyone else are looking out for me.

As I stand in *la madrina*'s doorway, I can't help but think about all the Mexicans who were new to the US, doing all the things that Americans take for granted, yet at the same time, walled off from the people around them. No invitations to dinner. No inquiries about where they are from or what they are doing here. No offers to show them around. No birth-day celebrations with seventeen strangers. I may have felt suffocated in *la madrina*'s house, but at least I wasn't alone in a strange country.

As I stepped out into the night, *la madrina* shouted to me, "Even if you decide not to live here, at least come for dinner every so often."

Sometimes I Feel My Gender

For two countries that share a border, Mexico and the United States differ very much in terms of culture. Not just the explicit things, such as food, sports, language, etc., but also in what is implicit as well—the aspects of society that can't be seen but which form the core of culture

Young drummers react to the camera in a downtown plaza, Querétaro.

that is difficult for outsiders to understand. It's the sense of time, the styles of communicating, and ways of relating to others. In the US, for example, I viewed myself as a fiercely independent woman, and that coming to Mexico was just another branch toward further self-reliance. Yet once I crossed the border into a new land, my sense of independence was throttled, mainly by the fact that as a woman, there were certain things I just couldn't do on my own. That shift in the ways I viewed and felt my gender was certainly the biggest adjustment for me, especially when I first arrived in Mexico.

Before living in Celaya, my gender had never been so interwoven into my everyday choices and thoughts—such as what to wear, whom to associate with, and how to deal with both friends and strangers. There were, of course, the uncomfortable interactions—the catcalls on the streets, the men in bars, the teenage boys who looked me up and down shamelessly. There was the elderly man whom I greeted with the standard "*buenas tardes*," who shot back, "*Hoooola muchacha guapa*," ("Hello, pretty girl") complete with a wink and puckered lips. I kept walking from him as if this was just another normal encounter. In both the United States and Mexico, it often is. The difference was that as a white woman coming to Mexico, I stood out. For the first time, I felt simultaneously objectified and exoticized as a woman.

However, such encounters were not actually what impacted me most as a woman in Mexico. When someone yelled at me on the street, I could retreat into the confines of my body—plant my feet firmly on the ground and stare straight ahead. My ability to ignore the passerby made me feel stronger. The greater challenge was making friends, given the fact that most of the attention came from older, single men, like Luis. He was far from the only one. There was a man I'll call Friend One, a fellow teacher who liked to go beyond the standard kiss greeting by planting his sloppy lips directly onto my cheek and lingering there. There was Friend Two, a French teacher who texted me every weekend wanting to go out and get drunk. There was Friend Three from dance class, who would sit in silence over dinner together but still be wounded when I was ready to leave. There was Friend Four, who called me most nights just to see what I was doing. And finally, Friend Five, who always put his arm around me on the bus ride home.

Of course, I could have declined just all these "friendly" invitations and stayed home with a good book and a big tub of pomegranate seeds. But as a stranger in a new country, I wanted and needed friends. I wanted to explore, but in a town touched by organized crime, I was not comfortable doing so on my own.

This dilemma crystallized during the celebration of Mexican Independence Day. As I sat on my bed, wondering how to fulfill my desire to participate in the celebration, I almost felt like I was back in high school, with that same sense of a looming weekend night without any plans. But I did have invitations to go places. I could go with Friend

Four to Querétaro and return by bus at three in the morning (when I informed Friend Four that that was too late for me, he made plans for us to stay at his aunt's house). Or I could spend the evening with Friend One's family at his church (likely a night full of slobbery cheek kisses). Or I could go to a dinner party at Friend Three's house: certainly the most benign option.

In Friend Three's living room, I stared blankly as he ate his pork skins and bemoaned his lot in life. It turned out that this little dinner party was more of a gathering for two, as his family was scattered about the house, involved in their own affairs. So I tried to get to know Friend Three with only a bit more effort than I put into picking at the pig's hoof on my plate. He was looking for a job, so I asked him what kind he hoped to find. He didn't know. I broached the subject of his open relationship with his girlfriend. Why hadn't he seen her in three months? He didn't know. I brought the conversation back to the one thing we had in common: dance class. Why had he decided to take the class? He didn't have anything better to do. This had been my best option for the night, yet I was already plotting how to politely find an alternative.

My escape came in the form of a text from a coworker asking me to go salsa dancing. When I invited Friend Three to join us, he responded, "But I thought we could go salsa dancing."

"Great, well then let's go."

"No," he retorted. "I thought *we* could go salsa dancing."

In the end, Friend Three did not want to come with us, and even worse, he refused to give me his address so that my coworker could pick me up. Instead, *he* wanted to take me to the bar, despite the fact that he didn't have a car and it made no sense to take the bus. But driving me did not have to do with practicality, but was rather a way for him to claim me, to assert that I had come to *his* house for dinner. I was not having it. I took a taxi.

"They see someone who doesn't matter to them."
Though I may have felt exposed at times walking down the street in Celaya or in interactions with older men, my privilege as a white woman and an American mitigated any real vulnerability that my gender might bring. I had options. The migrant women I interviewed lacked any such latitude.

In a 2010 report, the Washington Office on Latin America documented Nancy's story. A twenty-four-year-old Salvadorian, Nancy was taking refuge at a shelter in Veracruz. "It was the supposed shelter of a woman nicknamed, 'the mother' who tried to pass for a nun so that we would trust her and fall into her trap," she recalled.[1] Then they came—Zeta kidnappers, who abducted her and eighty-three others. They shoved the victims in trucks and took them to Reynosa, Tamaulipas, near the border. On the way there, the kidnappers repeatedly raped Nancy and the other women. When a male companion tried to protect them, he was in turn raped and beaten to death. The trucks passed through several INM and *federales* checkpoints, but the kidnappers paid off the officials and went through without consequence.

In Reynosa, the Zetas demanded ransom, while continuing to rape the women and batter the men. Two women in the group paid the ransom, were set free, and decided to turn themselves in to the Mexican immigration authorities, since there was no way they could continue the journey. The corrupt officials sold them right back to the Zetas, who dragged them back to the same house where Nancy was being held. In a particularly gruesome spectacle, the kidnappers murdered the women and displayed their bodies for Nancy and the rest of the hostages. "The kidnappers made all of us kneel in front of the alter with the two women's bodies there to ask forgiveness from the Santa Muerte," Nancy attested.[2]

"During all of this time, three Mexican men, who were the bosses, would often come to look for the women that were there so they could sexually abuse us," Nancy recollected. "The three of them raped me several times." Eventually, the kidnappers asked Nancy to work for them, helping "bring them people" from El Salvador. Thinking it might be a way out of that haunted room, Nancy at first agreed. "Then I got scared and I told them no." Fortunately, Nancy's aunt scrounged together enough ransom to get her out, allowing her to decline their offer. "Fifteen days after she deposited the money that they asked for, they set me free."

Sadly, Nancy's horrific story is not uncommon, as rape and sexual assault are nauseatingly familiar on the journey north. It is extremely difficult to get an exact number of affected women, as reporting systems are faulty and the stigma around sexual violence prevents many women from coming forward. However, based on reports from social workers and shelter directors, there are estimates that as many as 80 percent of women are sexually assaulted at some point on the migrant trail.[3] Hugo, the director of Celaya's long-term shelter, had an even higher estimate—90 percent—based on the women coming through his shelter over its five years in operation. (The situation was grave enough that the shelter hired an on-call psychologist specifically to counsel these women.) These numbers are astounding, indicating that only a small minority avoid this agonizing trauma. The rest are made to "pay with their bodies," as Lucy, one migrant woman, was told when men forced her to work at a brothel.[4] Women often have no choice but to submit, as their attackers often weld physical or logistical power over them.

Kidnappers, random criminals, *polleros,* Mexican officials, and

American border patrol agents have all raped women as they move north.[5] Just as with migrant kidnappings, most of these men get away with their crimes. The stories abound. In 2016, a smuggler raped two migrant women in a stash house along the border, leaving one of them pregnant. In 2017, a *pollero* raped a Salvadorian woman twice while crossing toward Arizona, threatening to leave her behind if she resisted his attacks. "I hope I leave you pregnant with one of my kids," the smuggler reportedly told her. In July 2019, another *coyote* raped a Honduran woman in a bedroom closet while her group waited to cross. In the south Texas desert, a *pollero* raped a thirty-nine-year-old woman, biting her mouth so she couldn't cry out for help.[6] These documented stories just scrape the surface.

In addition to the criminals and *polleros*, Mexican and American officials also prey on migrant women. As sociologist Sylvanna Falcón explains, rape is about power and is often deployed as a weapon of war to dehumanize victims.[7] Indeed, with the militarization of the border—as well as the migrant routes across Mexico—immigration officials often view these women as the enemy and thus feel justified in completely disregarding their humanity. In one ghastly 2014 case, Esteban Manzanares, a Border Patrol agent, drove a mother and two teenage girls to an isolated area outside of McAllen, Texas after they had surrendered to immigration. He then slashed the mother and daughter's wrists, twisted their necks, and raped the other teenage girl. He left the first two to bleed out, while tying the remaining girl to a tree where he duct-taped her mouth. He headed back to the station, clocked out, and then collected the girl from the tree to bring her to his apartment. There, Manzanares tied her to his bed and continued to rape her. When agents closed in for his arrest, he shot himself in the apartment, his victim still tied to the bed.[8] While this example is extreme, it points to a larger issue: the nature of the Border Patrol's work leaves agents in unsupervised remote locations while interacting with the most vulnerable populations.

Similarly, in detention centers, abuses are also widespread. From October 2014 to July 2018, the Office of Refugee Resettlement received 4,556 allegations of sexual assault or harassment of minors in federally funded detention centers.[9] While this number includes allegations of attacks perpetrated by other minors, it does not incorporate the number of adults assaulted—nor the innumerable unreported cases.

In Mexico, sexual crimes and rape by corrupt officials is perhaps even more rampant than with the US Border Patrol, as there are few mechanisms to prevent abuses in the Instituto Nacional de Migración (as discussed in Chapter Nine). Alejandro Vila, head of the special prosecutor's office in Chiapas, a rare unit charged with investigating crimes against migrants in the state, acknowledged that officer abuse is a major issue. "We have active cases here of officials who've been detained and are facing criminal proceedings . . . for abusing the vulnerable migrant women specifically." Vila continued, "Of course we know about this—how could we not? There are cases where women offer their bodies in exchange for being able to cross over."[10]

Vila also noted that for "women crossing alone, the risk of becoming a crime victim increases significantly."[11] This holds true all the way to the border, where US policies exacerbate women's exposure. For instance, the Alien Transfer Exit Program (ATEP), launched in 2008, laterally deports migrants to a different area than their point of entry. Under this program, women have frequently been sent to different locations along the border than their husbands or male traveling companions, to erode their social capital and theoretically prevent them from crossing again. One woman affected by this program, María, was deported to Nogales while authorities sent her husband elsewhere. She had no idea where he was or how to contact him. Eventually, she discovered that he had been relocated to Tijuana. María and her daughter begged for money for weeks to raise enough bus fare to meet him. During this period, she was solicited for sex work several times.[12] While a male companion by no means guarantees safety, being alone is certainly worse. Immigration policies that specifically alienate female migrants are actively exposing them to sexual assault.

Many women who travel through Mexico and across the border take birth control pills to avoid pregnancy should they be raped.[13] This is a tragic trade-off. To make it across the border, women literally have to accept and prepare for the eventuality that they'll experience a life-altering trauma. "It wasn't me anymore," one migrant mourned, after she was forced into prostitution. "I think since they put me in that room, they killed me . . . They don't see that you're a mother, that you have family. They see someone who doesn't matter to them."[14]

The Twenty-Three-Year-Old Expert

"Oh, we forgot to tell Kelsey," the English program coordinator at the university where I taught announced in an impromptu meeting. Not a good sign.

"What do you need?" I asked cheerily, trying to maintain my air of "always willing to help," when I was dreading yet another assignment for which I was not qualified.

"Remember we're having our end-of-the-semester event on Friday. Students are going to share their work and parents will be there and we're inviting the mayor and people from the newspaper. We put you down as the MC of the event. You're okay with that, right?"

His "right?" cut off any opportunity I had to say no. So instead I tentatively replied, "I can do that," with big pauses in between each word. "But why would you want me to introduce all these projects? I only have a faint idea of what students are doing in other classes and I'm sure I'll make mistakes with my Spanish."

"Well I think the parents would really like to see you involved."

"Besides, you can do it in English if you want," another teacher chimed in. This seemed impractical given that most of the audience wouldn't understand me. "You are our English master," the teacher continued. Language was not the problem. I actually enjoyed public speaking in Spanish and could add commentary to the program. My hesitation instead stemmed from the obvious fact that I was the least qualified person to represent the school in front of parents and city officials. I had only been in Celaya for three months. I had only just figured out that mechatronics (one of the university's three majors) had something to do with robotics, mechanics, and computer science. Apparently, some students took Japanese classes on Saturdays—another recently discovered secret. In preparation for this end of semester event, students had been spending hours building miniature replicas of the Eiffel Tower out of bottle caps and duct tape. Did I have any idea why? No.

I knew why they wanted me to MC. It was the same reason they would periodically cancel my classes to send me to college fairs around the city (despite the fact that I knew next to nothing about the university). I was white and American, and thus brought this exotic air of internationalism that the school could use to burnish its image—"the parents will appreciate it."

When I studied abroad as an undergraduate in Yucatán, Mexico, I conducted a community-based project on Mayan education. While digging through the nuances of Indigenous relations in Mexico, I began to see firsthand which groups were associated with success and which were stereotyped with backwardness. I worked at a Mayan preschool in the rural village of Canicab, and in subtle and blatant ways, western values, people, and modes of thought were exhibited as the exemplary models to follow. While pictures of white cartoon characters brushing their teeth and behaving well were plastered on the walls of this designated Indigenous school, the hashtag *Es de indios,* (meaning "that's so Indian,") paired with backward or out of style situations circulated on Twitter (as in, "That's so Indian to use Facebook.") There is a hierarchy of cultures, colors and races in Mexico. Suddenly I found that my barely adult voice was afforded more weight that it merited—than it would have had if I was not a white American.

In Celaya, I was certainly never treated as a second-class citizen. On the contrary, there were several instances when—despite being just out of college with very little experience—I was suddenly viewed as the expert. I thought of my friends in New York or Boston beginning their internships, where the most responsibility granted to them might be writing an important email. At the university, however, I was solicited for advice on subjects ranging from teaching styles to phonetics instruction. Once, when passing by my supervisor's desk, he asked me to take a look at a new month-long Spanish language program he had designed. "I'm planning on spending a week on phonetics, two weeks on grammar, and a week on communication at the end. What do you think?"

"Well," I offered, "when I learned Spanish, we never even focused on phonetics. We concentrated more on grammar structures and speaking and listening. I think through these exercises, we just acquired proper pronunciation over time." I was quick to emphasize, "I'm not saying that's the way it has to be. That's just how I learned."

In a matter of minutes, he had altered his program to include just one activity focused on phonetics, beginning the course with a greater focus on grammar, speaking, and listening. I was astounded. Why didn't he ask Agustin, a teacher who wrote his thesis on bilingual education, or Gloria, who had over twenty-five years of experience teaching English? Instead, he sought out my amateur advice, and immediately took it to heart. With my whiteness lingering in people's consciousness, I was automatically assumed to be the expert.

The most blatant example of my undeserved stature came just before the teachers were scheduled to have a training day—meaning they would have to come in on a national holiday to listen to presentations about pedagogy. A few days before the training, the language coordinator asked me to speak. Since it was early in the semester, I was less disillusioned and genuinely enthusiastic about the invitation. But about what? "We would love it if you talk about how you see the university."

I pondered this broad and inherently problematic assignment, and then responded, "What exactly do you mean?"

"You know, tell us how you see things here. What do you think works well? What should we do differently? How do you think the students are doing?" He read the hesitation printed on my face and offered, "You can speak in English if you want," as if using my native language would ameliorate the difficulty of the topic. With no visible way to get out of it, I agreed.

For two days before the training, I stressed about the speech. It was as if my boss had just handed me a white savior hat to put on. In the end, I did not talk about my perceptions of the university. Instead, I used the time to clarify my role as an assistant, emphasize that I was not an expert, and offer a few observations as an outsider, not an authority.

As this story of white American privilege played out at my

workplace, I thought of Roberto, a Salvadorian migrant who we met earlier in the book, and whose story we will discuss in more detail in the next chapter. With a degree in computer science, he was heading north, willing to take whatever work he could get. "I'll take a job scrubbing toilets, and I'll be so happy to just have a job," he told me as we spoke on a rainy afternoon. Unlike the way my Mexican colleagues viewed me, he knew that Americans would not see him as the expert in his field, though he in fact was; the power structures would not work in his favor.

At my desk, as a sixty-year-old professor asked me how to teach "didactic texts." I pictured Roberto, wherever he might be, and wondered what kinds of questions would be placed before him.

Eleven

CHRONICLES OF POST-ELECTION DAYS IN MEXICO

DURING THE LEAD-UP TO THE 2016 US presidential election, it was impossible to ignore the atmosphere of fear that the candidacy of Donald Trump inspired among Mexicans. Almost every day, someone would ask me about the election, usually by tentatively inquiring about who I was voting for. It was then my task to explain why my country would support a man who continuously and unabashedly degraded Mexicans. Over and over again, I had to look people in the eye and try to unpack the hate that the Trump candidacy had unleashed among so many Americans.

I would start by expressing my utter disappointment in many of my fellow Americans, then try to instill some optimism. Trump's going to lose, I would predict. Excessive media attention (due to his outrageous discourse and extremism) had sensationalized his beliefs. I'd explain how many voters, excluded from primary elections, were moderate, and therefore would offset the extremists lining up to vote for Trump in the general election. And besides, Hillary Clinton was leading in the polls. Things would turn out alright, I assured them.

Then I'd switch to a softer tone, mentioning how there was a significant portion of the US population that was incredibly frustrated with the current state of politics. These people were mainly working class and white, a group that was understandably uncertain about their future economic stability. It was easy to capitalize on their disappointment and fear and redirect it toward immigrants, Muslims, and foreigners. I would tell them that Donald Trump was cultivating this anxiety and placing the blame on immigrants (among others) to bolster his own platform. Blame and racist discourse is an easy way to gain quick attention, but I had faith that my country would reject it in the upcoming election.

This was my narrative. I repeated it so often during the run-up to the election that I almost believed it would come true. Of course, America was better than the inanity we were currently witnessing. But as I'd repeat these sentences to my students, fellow teachers, or random people, there was a piece of me that could never fully rationalize Trump. I could logically understand his appeal, but there was always a strand of me that could never comprehend how anyone—especially a presidential nominee—could be so callously blind to the consequences of their words. And that, worse still, a great many people seemed to feel that this was acceptable.

Speaking about people who I would have never imagined would be okay with Trump's rhetoric, about a month before the election, I had a debate with a Mexican Trump supporter (rare, but they do exist). His support for Trump was grounded in economics, and while I challenged his stance on issues like taxation and trade, I tried to steer the conversation back to Trump's hateful rhetoric. How could this man support someone who had said such disparaging things about Mexicans? He dodged the question and relentlessly asserted the sexist notion that Trump was stronger, and thus a better leader.

I later speculated on how this man could ignore Trump's blatant racism. Perhaps when Trump declared that Mexico sent "the bad ones over because they don't want to pay for them. They don't want to take care of them," this man (who had studied in Chicago) did not see himself in these words. [1] Or when Trump condoned the beating of a Latino man in Boston by saying the perpetrators were "very passionate. They love this country and they want it to be great again," maybe this man could not relate to being terrorized merely because of his nationality.[2] Perhaps this man could dismiss Trump's words with a simple, "Well, he doesn't mean me."

But what if you were a migrant from Mexico? What if you did not enjoy the privilege of saying that Trump's bigotry didn't apply to you? What was it like to carry not only the weight of the tumultuous experience of migrating, but also of Trump's (and all his supporters') words? In a 2016 article, journalist Declan Walsh interviewed a border resident near Nogales, Arizona, who argued that Navy SEALS with AR-15 rifles should patrol the border and shoot anyone that crossed.[3] As a migrant, what must it feel like to hear someone plainly state that you should be killed, to have your life utterly invalidated like that?

I spoke with dozens of Mexicans and Central Americans who were frightened and offended by the words of the man who would become the President of the United States. Some were migrants, still heading north despite deep uncertainty about the politics to come. Others had friends or family in the US and were worried that their loved ones would be personally targeted. Others were students, who could not comprehend the racist discourse coming from a country that supposedly championed human rights—or at least had in the past.

Worlds Between Us

"They need us, but they don't want us," Roberto bemoaned, his eyes looking down toward the concrete floor. A Salvadorian migrant in his late thirties, Roberto had tight black curls and a strong jawline. He had never been to the US before, but even from the shelter in Celaya, he was certainly not naive about what it would mean to be an undocumented worker.

"Give me a job," he said, looking up and staring me straight in the face, "a job that you would never do. Cleaning toilets? Would you clean toilets for a living?"

"Not if I had another option," I answered.

"And what's the minimum wage in the US?"

"Depends on the state, but between $7.25 and $15 per hour."

"So, would you clean toilets for $5 an hour?"

"No."

"You see I would. I would take that job and I would be happy with it because I don't have another option."

Roberto was keenly aware that migrating to the U.S would mean taking any job, being paid below minimum wage, and working obscene hours, despite the fact that he had a degree in computer science. It was simply because of his nationality and undocumented status. He threw out these callous truths as proof that what the immigrant experience meant depended on where you came from. He mentioned that, near the Mexico-Guatemalan border, he and two other migrants had been offered a job unloading cement trucks for 200 pesos per day. Split between the three of them, this sum amounted to approximately $3 daily. As he noted, being undocumented in another country always entails being taken advantage of by employers. You need work, so you scrub toilets for $5 an hour. You do jobs that others (like me) would never do to fuel a country that portrays you as a criminal. "This is called exploitation," Roberto remarked. "But it's also called 'thank God I have a job.'"

A few days before I spoke with Roberto, I had awoken to a Facebook message from my aunt. She had read an interview I had posted with a migrant at the shelter. "You have a very compassionate heart," she began. "But I would like you to consider that there are other stories just as heartbreaking on this side of the border. Stories of hardships created or amplified because we are not taking care of our own citizens. As a part of the current immigration policy they are being given housing and other benefits that people who are natural born citizens don't have . . . Sort of like if in your own family you didn't have some of your basic needs met but your parents were going to pay for college education for ten complete strangers, and if you want to go to college you have to figure out some other way."

The message reminded me that combatting xenophobia was about more than asking people to empathize with the experiences of immigrants. It was also about debunking the "it's either us or them" narrative. I understood my aunt's words, and saw the frustration threaded in the white spaces between them. Disheartened and tired of the status quo, many conclude that immigrants are benefitting from our programs, while citizens are not. But it's not a simple trade-off. Undocumented immigrants like Roberto do the jobs that form the backbone of the US economy—jobs that most citizens will not do for so little money—not to mention the taxes they pay and the benefits they lack. It's called exploitation, but it's also called, "thank God we can fill those jobs."

"If I could ever get a work visa to the US for just six months, I would follow all the rules down to the last detail," Roberto continued. "But there just aren't enough visas. So you have to go illegally. And the moment you enter the country, you're already a criminal."

Roberto certainly did not present like a criminal. His manner of speaking was both articulate and direct, and he did not let me meander around the sharp realities of his story. He tapped his heel against the linoleum floor as he spoke, emanating a persistent sense of anxiety. As with all at the shelter, he appeared to be exhausted.

Twenty-four days before I spoke with Roberto in Celaya, he had left San Salvador with a backpack and $120. "It hurt so much to leave them," he said, referring to his girlfriend and daughter. "It hurts me here." He rested his hand above his heart. I thought he might cry. The tears never came, but the undeniable anguish in his voice spoke volumes. "I talked to my mom for the first time yesterday. There was no way to contact anyone before. And she was just crying and crying because she didn't even know if I was alive. And we talked for three free minutes before I had to hang up."

As we saw in chapter two, Roberto had begun his journey north by traveling on the infamous *bestia*. But after crossing the Mexico-Guatemalan border, he was on the train for just twenty minutes when *la migra* arrived. Bolting the scene, Roberto scurried through the brush until he could be sure that he wasn't being followed. For the next twelve days, he walked across southern Mexico, pulling his backpack straps toward his sternum to help ease the weight. "I didn't know anyone," he recalled. "I slept in the streets and there were six days where I barely slept at all. I went days without eating." Then he turned to address the other shelter occupants in the room. "How many of you have eaten something every day that you've been out here?" They looked around uncertainly. Some shook their heads. "No one?" he persisted.

"No one," someone replied out of the dark corner.

Roberto turned back to back to me. "You see. Have you ever gone a day without eating?" It was not a question out of malice, but merely a way to point out the different realms we occupied.

When I first started spending time at the migrant shelter, I tended to underemphasize my privilege as a white American. I would not mention my weekend travels around Mexico or other pleasure trips, as if hiding these luxuries could somehow dampen the migrants' burdens of the journey north. Over time, however, I realized that by owning my privilege, I could start to break down the walls between the two worlds. "No. I've been lucky enough to never go hungry." Roberto nodded.

We moved on to his hopes for life in the United States. He was planning to head to Los Angeles, but when I asked him why, he did not have an answer. "It's a place I know of," he stated plainly, then added, "I don't know. I don't really know where I'm going. I know I'll suffer in the United States. Even though it's the greatest power in the world, I'll suffer. It's just so hard to be stable without papers there. Even with the idea of not having anyone to lend me a hand, I suffer."

We spoke about the different regions of the US, and his interest in Colorado grew as I spoke about the state. By the end, he had changed his destination to Denver. I pressed a piece of paper in his palm with my Facebook info and promised to send him the names and addresses of organizations that could help him once he arrived in the city.

"I want to write a book," he declared. "A book about all my experiences. And you'll definitely appear in the book."

"You really should. You should share your story. You have so much to tell people who don't understand immigration."

A few days later, when I sent Roberto some Denver-based immigrant organizations via Facebook, he seemed utterly astounded that I had actually followed up. Over the next week, he sent me updates about where he was. One day he sent a message that read, "*Hola ya estoy en frontera d ee. Uu le hablo cuAndo esté.*" Crossing the border. I sat in a café in Celaya's ritziest neighborhood, the worlds between Roberto and I growing. Even from this physical and economical distance, my heart clenched. I would wait for the message saying he was in Denver, knowing that it might never come.

Election Day(s)

I had gone to bed before the results were finalized, but I already knew who had won. In the shadows of my gray bedroom the next morning, I reflected upon our attempts over the past half century to dig our way out of the muddy trench of bigotry. While we continuously slid backward, at least we were trying to advance. As the clock ticked in an otherwise silent room, I remind myself that Trump would be president, and I felt as though America had finally let go and fallen into the hole.

The night before, I had watched as one state, then another, turned red on my phone screen. Eventually, I couldn't take it anymore, and put the phone away. My roommate, Pablo, assured me that the world would still turn tomorrow. It wasn't over, he reminded me. Yet as more states turned red behind the black of my turned-off phone screen, it felt like much more of an injustice than just losing an election. It was the validation of bigotry.

Later that morning, I take my seat on the bus and pondered the task ahead of me: to explain all that happened, and why, to my Mexican students and colleagues. Yet as I enter the university and shamble to my desk, contrary to my expectations, all eyes aren't on me demanding an explanation. School life continues.

"Kelseys!!!" A coworker acknowledges my presence with his standard exuberant greeting (which always included adding an "S" onto my name) and a fist bump. "How are you Kelseys?"

"Well, honestly kind of bad."

"Bad? Kelseys is bad? Why Kelseys?"

"Because of the US election."

"Oh yeah, that Trump won," he said, rounding his English words together. We both pause, letting all that that means sink in. "Well don't worry Kelseys. *Hay que seguir adelante.*" We have to keep going.

I shoot an email to a close friend in Guadalajara, expressing dismay. She responds immediately: "Maybe this feeling is a bit more normal for me since each election is basically the same. It seems incredible to me that people exist that agree with such abhorrent proposals and with a party that is basically corrupt in essence." Whether she is talking about America or Mexico, it doesn't matter. The sentiment applies to both countries. "My outlook and that of my people is not very hopeful . . . My president is an idiot, manipulator, and a coward. Yours is a shark." Yes, of course this is not new for Mexicans who, at the time, had a president who had plagiarized his law thesis and allegedly ordered the crackdown and rape of protestors in Atenco when he was governor there. How could a man like that become the President of Mexico? How could Trump become President of the United States? The more I spoke with people of color about the election back in the States, the more I understood that of course the validation of bigotry was nothing new for them either. "I'm not surprised," a friend told me. "This is the America I have always known."

A little while later, my boss comes in to inform me that he's going to cover my class that afternoon, as I will be going to another college fair instead. I am relieved that I do not have to face the students—I am too worn down to set an optimistic example for how we can move forward just yet. An hour later, I find myself standing behind a booth, handing out brochures about the university. I spout the things I am told to say, a mind-numbing task that makes me feel like a cog in a machine on a dreary day.

Later that afternoon, when I drop off my laundry, the wash lady asks me what I think about Trump. *"Es un horror."* These words signal that I am on her side. *"Solo Dios nos puede ayudar,"* she tells me as I walk out the door. *Only God can help us now.* I step over a dead crow on the sidewalk.

The day after Election Day. I wake up, and for a moment focus on the day ahead. Then I remember. Gloom returns. In class, I project visualizations of election outcomes on a white board. What happened? The electoral college; swing states; more working-class white men voting than ever before; less people of color voting than during the Obama elections; 46 percent of the country not voting at all; the industrial Midwest swinging right; and so on. Most students express worry for their families in the US.

One student has a question, but is hesitant to ask it. I urge her forward. "Do you think that Trump will allow people to go around killing Mexicans?" she finally begins. "It's just that I saw this movie where there were designated times for hunting Mexicans. Do you think something like that will happen?" The fear etched on her face is hauntingly real. Even if no physical aggression materializes against Mexicans north of the border, there is already a sense of violence in the air.

Two days after the election. Around 9pm, I force myself to go out with my roommate. We sit in the dim light of a bar called Wings Army, a place that is decorated with pictures of Uncle Sam, camouflage, and American army relics. A live band belts out bad rock music in English.

"Why do you feel like you need to represent your country?" my roommate Pablo shouts over the din, cradling his Indio brand beer.

I tell him about the purpose of my Fulbright, about promoting cultural exchange.

"Yeah, I guess," he responds. "But when I was in Germany, my grant was focused on cultural exchange too, but I didn't feel like I needed to be a representative of Mexico. I think there's more to it for you."

From the corner of the bar, Uncle Sam's black eyes press into me, and his index finger remains perpetually extended in my direction.

"I guess I don't so much feel like a representative of my country," I tell him. "No person can truly represent a whole country because it's just too diverse. But I do feel like I have a huge opportunity to break a lot of stereotypes that people hold, even if in small ways. I think my job is not so much to represent, but to expose nuances, especially at a time when the US just seems like a homogenous mass of racism. People need to hear voices that stand up against bigotry, so that they don't meet this hate with more waves of hate toward all Americans."

The bad rock song ends, and the lead singer presses his lips into the microphone and shouts, "*¡Qué muera Trump!*" *Down with Trump.* Uncle Sam still glowers at me.

Three days after the election. A coworker who works for an exchange program asks me to talk about the election at their monthly employee conference. As I await my turn to speak, I listen to the employees stress the importance of cultural exchange and the free flow of ideas. "In 2017, we're going to focus on sending more students to Canada," one presenter says, "instead of the United States." She glances apologetically in my direction. I don't blame her. But as the conference continues, I think about what it means that America will be losing students because of its racist discourse. And with these channels severed, the US will also be losing the ideas and nuances about other countries that these exchanges bring. Our slide toward bigotry seems like a feedback loop: as we exude hatred into the world, we cut ourselves off from the possibility to truly connect and learn about each other.

Moments before I stand to speak, I remind myself that I am an individual. I can choose where I fit in to the picture and progress of my country. The election of Trump is not the end of the story. So I stand to tell a different story. "*Soy Kelsey, y soy de Estados Unidos*," I begin.

Juxtapositions

"If the tables were turned, Americans would not hesitate to hate all Mexicans." I listened to these words and they weighed more heavily in my stomach than the fourth powdered sugar cookie I was eating. I was listening to a presentation from a fellow Fulbright scholar, during our midyear reunion in Baja California. She was speaking about how, if a Mexican president (and his supporters) were imparting the same kind of hatred-laden, blanket statements toward Americans that Trump was blurting out about Mexicans, Americans surely would retaliate with hatred toward Mexicans in the United States. However, in the months after Trump was elected, not a single Mexican person had conflated me with his America or met me with any kind of hatred. Instead, they politely asked me many questions, allowing me to share a different story about my country. They were able to separate me from my ugly government. So why, despite every example of how massing people under blanket stereotypes has gone awry, do we still, *still*, follow these same patterns in the US?

The bulk of the reunion focused on intercultural communication, which stood in stark contrast to the dark Trump world that was forming outside the walls of the fancy hotel. During one workshop, cross-cultural expert Mary Ellen Colon emphasized that, "We are at a point in our history where there are more of us thrown together than ever before, whether because of technology, globalization, migration or social media. But cultural understanding isn't a given simply by being in the same vicinity," a statement which was being proven in the US right at that moment. Mary Ellen went on to talk about implicit culture, which are the values that are imbedded within us from the time we're young. She spoke about individualism and collectivism by offering an example. "How does a mother in the US teach her baby how to walk?" We let the question settle among the sixty of us in silence, given our limited baby-raising knowledge. "She sets her down, steps away, and from a distance says 'Okay honey now stand up! Come toward me! You can do it! Here you go!' When the baby stands up on her own, she's met with praise." Right from the beginning, Americans are implanted with the idea that we should be independent, that doing things on your own is the best way.

"But how does a Mexican mom teach her baby to walk?" Mary Ellen asked. "She holds her hands, walks with her, and says 'mira, aquí estoy mija.' She's teaching that baby a certain interconnectedness, the idea that she'll always be there for her child." I began to see how various aspects of any particular culture complement each other. In Mexico, you walk with the help of your mother's hands, you leave the house when you're married, and you prioritize a conversation or helping a family member over arriving to the next thing exactly on time.

As these cultural cogs began to click into place for me inside the hotel, understanding was not the norm outside. Outside, refugees, green-card holders, and other authorized immigrants were being detained in airports because of a blanket travel ban against their country. Nazanin Zinouri, a recent Clemson University PhD graduate, had been removed from her flight to the US. Zinouri had returned to Tehran to visit her family, but booked a flight back to the US a few hours after she received word of Trump's immigration ban. After living in the US for seven years, she was detained upon her arrival in Washington, DC. "No one warned me when I was leaving, no one cared what will happen to my dog or my job or my life there," she said. "No one told me what I should do with my car that is still parked at the airport parking. Or what to do with my house and all my belongings. They didn't say it with words but with their actions, that my life doesn't matter. Everything I worked for all these years doesn't matter."[4]

Making sense of this juxtaposition between the utter invalidation of Muslim and Mexican lives in the US and the bright and socially conscious faces around me was like trying to force together two mismatched puzzle pieces. It felt impossible to reconcile these two versions of America in my mind; no matter how hard I shoved, the pieces wouldn't fit together.

Classroom Heartbreak

It was 3:20 PM on a Thursday afternoon, ten minutes into a class that I normally had with fifteen advanced English students. Today, there were only two students sitting in front of me, Lili and Melissa. *Well, that's better than yesterday, when no one showed up to class,* I thought. I started to connect the projector to the computer, trying to continue with my normal lesson plan with only two students. Then came a question from Lili: "Do you think there's more racism in the US now that Trump is elected?"

I paused, strolled over to where the two girls were seated, and placed myself gingerly in the seat in front of them. "Honestly, I think the racism we're seeing today in the US certainly existed before, but that Trump has given voice to that hatred. It's almost as if he's 'legit-imized' their racism because people begin to think, 'Well, if some-one in the most powerful post in the world can stereotype and hate Mexican immigrants, why should we hold back?' It's scary, but it was there before."

Lili kneaded over my answer in her mind. She was exceptionally bright, the kind of student who always came to class, asked interesting questions, and even borrowed a new novel in English from me a week after she had checked out the last one from the library. "It's just that I've seen so many videos on the Internet where Mexicans or Black people are getting beat up because of their race," she said. "And now my parents say that if they put me in United States instead of Canada, I have to say I can't go." Several students in the class, including Lili, were prepping to study abroad in Canada or the States the following year through a pres-tigious scholarship program. I knew what the opportunity meant to her. She shouldn't have to give it up.

I responded by emphasizing how these racist acts seemed more common than they were because of the rapid diffusion of information via social media. Since these were the main stories coming out of the US in the wake of Trump's election, of course it appeared like every-one in the country was a practicing racist. "My parents were also afraid for me to go to Mexico because the stories that reach the US are almost entirely about drug cartels, violence, widespread disappearances, mur-ders," I added. "So, when that's all you hear, you think that everywhere in Mexico is overridden with violence. But then you get here and you realize that's not the case. Yes, there are hate crimes happening in the US, but they are by no means the norm."

Lili looked down, her face still creased with worry. My comparison was not totally off base; yes, stories have the power to distort the image of a nation. But our parents' fears were different. Mine were afraid I would be kidnapped because it's more common in Mexico; Lili's parents were afraid that she would be singled out and assaulted *specifically because of her race.* Racially targeted violence (even just verbal violence) cuts to the core of who you are, twisting up your gut in indignation and fear at the cruelty of the world.

I shifted to focusing on how hate crimes hadn't been the only response to Trump's election. I talked about the Women's March on Washington, how only 46 percent of Americans had even voted, and that less than half of that percentage voted for Trump. And out of those that voted for Trump, not everyone did so because they espoused racist views of Mexicans or thought we should deport all illegal immigrants. I explained to her how some people compartmentalized Trump's views on immigration or his discourse toward women from his views on economic policy, for instance. They may not have agreed with things he said, but they voted for him anyway. In my view, I told them, by voting for Trump, you were condoning his racism and sexism and there was no separating those views from other policies. But that wasn't the case for everyone.

After my little pep talk, Lili and Melissa seemed a tad less upset, but certainly not settled. They didn't understand Trump. They didn't understand why he would suddenly devote so much money to deporting people who were working hard and supporting their families. They couldn't comprehend why he would ban so many Muslim refugees when the US had played a role in creating violence in their countries in the first place. As a teacher, I was impressed by their knowledge of US politics and their ability to pinpoint these contradictions.

I tucked my palms under my thighs and sat up a little straighter. I wanted to footnote our conversation with something positive. "Plus,"

I added, "It's such an important time to be in the US and share all you have to offer. Here, when I become so disheartened by all that's happening in my country, I try to remind myself that now, more than ever, it's a crucial time to show that Americans are more than Trump's news stories. I do think that that type of cross-cultural exchange has so much power. Maybe you'll meet some American friend that didn't know much about Mexico before and was somewhat indifferent to Trump's immigration policies. But just by meeting you and hearing your experiences, that friend changes her perspective. That's something really powerful that you can do just by being you."

Even after this attempt to end our conversation on an up note, there was still a pronounced uneasiness swimming in my stomach. After all, I hadn't been to the US since August, so what did I really know about what was happening there. One big question crossed my mind: Was the country that had nurtured me, protected me, and given me amazing opportunities still capable of doing the same for people like Lili and Melissa?

Dreams Made in Mexico

"I feel like since moving here, I don't know if it's because of the type of school I'm at or because I don't feel like anything's holding me back anymore, but I'm definitely dreaming a lot higher, and I think I will be doing a lot more important things . . . I think that's the biggest effect that moving here has had on me."

Sergio Ocampo Estrada sat across from me at a fancy French café in Querétaro, stirring his French onion soup in circular swirls. Soft classical music padded the space around us, and the intense May sunlight washed over the room. Sergio was not alluding to the "American Dream" as he spoke; rather, he was referencing his move to Mexico. He was from Rome, Georgia, and his parents had migrated to the US from Guerrero just before he was born. At eighteen, Sergio had decided to move to Querétaro to study international business, leaving his family back in Georgia. Two years had passed since his move, and he no longer felt like he was being held back. In the US, he continued, "You just kind of dream as big as what's around you. I mean I didn't really have a dream, just to kind of do a better job and try to move up." He prodded his spoon at the floating onions in his soup as he spoke.

Sergio was certainly the type of twenty-year-old that looked like he would succeed. His neatly trimmed, black hair rolled to the left in orderly waves, and his square-framed glasses gave him an air of intellectualism that all academics strive to emulate. A thin beard dotted his chin and cheeks. His friendly grin folded his cheeks into slight dimples at the tips of his mustache. As we sat down to eat, he began to divulge his newfound love for a podcast I had previously recommended to him. He picked apart the details of the latest episode for me. "You changed my life!" he exclaimed, flashing an endearing smile. Bright, eager, and confident, it surprised me that Sergio's dreams were not limitless, having grown up in the US.

"What was holding you back in the US?" I inquired.

"I am Hispanic, and I have to succeed to an extent. But what that means over there is graduating college, and whatever I do after that, it's like a success story." It was not as if Sergio's parents didn't support him or hope for great things for him. But the subtle messaging whispered by American society—in everything from advertisements to newspaper articles—seemed to set the bar for success at college for him. If you're white, like me, you might internalize a different message. You see your race represented in every field, so when you see someone like yourself writing a book, or running for office, or managing a non-profit, it doesn't seem infeasible for you to do the same. Perhaps you start to dream a little.

But it's easiest to start imagining such dreams after they are planted in your head. For Sergio, the seeds for more "out of proportion dreams" were sown in Mexico, not the US. "Here," Sergio shared, "at least with the people I'm surrounded by, you're expected to go to college and you're expected to do something greater . . . Certain people maybe grow up with that, like if you live in Palo Alto and are wealthy, but the rest of us in the US, you know, you just got to do what you got to do."

Since arriving in Querétaro, while Sergio would occasionally note some pop culture tidbit or local knowledge that he lacked, overall, he hardly ever felt like an outsider. In fact, he believed that his foreign perspective was respected and valued. "Since I got here, it's not like people see me as an immigrant," he told me. "It's been such a positive reception that it almost motivates you to be like 'hey, I'm doing something right.'" He mentioned one particular instance in his statistics class, where, since he had taken stats in high school, he already knew how to do some of the problems the class was working on. "I would do it just a little bit different than the teacher . . . and they'd celebrate that. They'd be like 'oh wow, that's an easier way, I'm going to do it this way.' Whereas in the US when an immigrant shows up it's like, "that's not the right way," because it's coming from a 'lesser place.'"

I thought back to my experiences as a student in the US. It was true—when a Mexican (or another immigrant) student suggested a new way to solve a problem that was based on what they did in their country, it was often shut down as "incorrect." After all, in the constructed hierarchy of world development, the US ranks on top. Why should methods from "underdeveloped" countries be considered when we supposedly already have the best possible way of doing things?

Thus, while Sergio internalized a "hey, I'm doing something right" message in Mexico, immigrant children in the US internalize "I'm wrong." And when you're "wrong" in school enough, you might start to question whether you're smart, whether you belong, whether you can succeed. As if to prove my point, Sergio added, "So that definitely gives me confidence."

And it isn't just in school. Immigrants on the whole often face a world where their expertise is automatically erased upon crossing the border. Both of Sergio's parents were in the US legally. Nevertheless, opportunities for them to work in their previous fields were limited. "My mom is a teacher and has a teaching degree in Mexico. My dad studied two years of accounting at one of the best universities in Mexico," Sergio recounted. Their professions, however, shifted upon coming to the US, their experience no longer valued in the way it might have been in Mexico.

"So why did you ultimately decide to come to Mexico?" I ventured.

Sergio slid his chair in toward the edge of the mahogany table. Even his slightest movements seemed to hold a tinge of politeness. "I had to be here eventually, and I knew that the older I got, the harder it would be." He flashed a smile. "I've always had a love for Mexico . . . just kind of the desire to live here because, I mean my parents are from here. I've come to visit, but only to see family." Sergio's connection to Mexico had obviously been cultivated by his parents, but by coming to Querétaro, he seemed to be forging his own relationship with its cultures, peoples, and places. He grew up speaking Spanish in his house, and he had always felt that he was Mexican. "(My parents) were never like 'be proud of who you are,'" he stated. "But they never gave me a reason not to be."

Sergio, more than I anyone I had met in the city, seemed to truly love Querétaro. "Isn't it such a beautiful city!" he had uttered as more statement than question on the night I met him. He seemed entranced. Querétaro does have a certain illustrious vibrancy to its historical buildings, hip cafes and illuminated churches. "This is what I imagine when I think of Mexico."

Although he was forming his own bond with Mexico, in a way, moving to Querétaro was a way of further connecting to his parents. "My dad lived in Mexico City when he went to college and he stayed at my godparents' house. And every time I go to Mexico City, I stay with them. And it's always so crazy to me that when my dad was my age, he lived here." Sergio's parents were also grateful that he had the opportunity to discover Mexico. His father was particularly proud. "They don't come from like, poor, I mean they always had something to eat," Sergio said. "But the fact that I had the opportunity to go to a school like Anáhuac, I guess he felt like he fulfilled his goals." Sergio's time in Querétaro also helped to reconnect his parents to Mexico. As soon as they retired, they were planning on moving back, mostly likely to Querétaro. "They've always wanted to come back to Mexico, and I feel like now I've given them a path . . . And that's something I'm really proud of because I want them to finally feel like they're home."

In the US, the general vision of Mexico is grossly incomplete. We think of Cancun and drunken beach parties, or, on the opposite end of the spectrum, the violence and drugs that have overtaken the *entire* country. Politically conscious whites with coexist bumper stickers chastise Trump because, after all, Mexican migrants are fleeing a horrible, chaotic, violent country. I myself have at times fallen victim to this narrative. But this is only one element of a much more nuanced story. Yes, Mexico has issues with political corruption and cartels and lack of economic opportunity and kidnappings and *femicidios* and police repression and suppression of speech. But it is also an indescribably beautiful country in terms of cultures, people, landscapes, ideas, and, for some, even opportunity. As Americans, we take the American Dream as a given, as if our reputation as the "land of opportunity" won't cease even with the hatred we espouse. But for my coworker Googling engineering jobs in Australia, America is not the land of opportunity. For my student who declined a scholarship to study in New York, America is not the land of opportunity. For Sergio, whose dreams took off when he left, America is not the land of opportunity. And for all the migrants that continue to head north, American may no longer be the beacon of hope that it once was—it's just a better option in a situation with dwindling choices.

Dancing *cumbia* in a Querétaro plaza.

PART FIVE

LEAVING THE SHELTER, COMING HOME

Twelve

LA DELINCUENCIA ON THE INSIDE

ALTHOUGH I COULD NEVER QUITE place my finger on it, something had always felt "off" about the migrant shelter in Celaya where I conducted most of my interviews. Maybe it was because they kept all the migrants locked in the front room—even to use the bathroom, you had to knock on a forbidding door that was patrolled by Lupita. Or maybe it was the day a sign was posted outside reading "closed for fumigation," yet Lupita still answered the intercom when I rang. Or the time I arrived to find a group of migrants waiting outside the shelter for four hours because Lupita had said that she needed to run an errand. Apparently, she had made all occupants leave, then never came back. When I called the director to see when Lupita was returning, I was met with a surprised (and over-eager), "Oh we'll be there in five minutes," and indeed they were. While these and many other facets of the shelter seemed odd, I initially cast them aside and assumed that the shelter still had the best interests of its transient population at heart. That is, until my meeting with Hugo.

Hugo was the director of the shelter I'll call *El Refugio*, the long-term migrant shelter in Celaya. The place could not have been more different from the other shelter. At *El Refugio*, the front door opened into a wide courtyard where children could play and adults could lounge.

Sunlight permeated the entire house. Plants, couches, and toys were stashed in the shade of the balcony, and the upstairs contained dormitories, a doctor's clinic, a psychiatrist's room, and ample space.

However, it was ultimately the volunteers that made this refuge feel so radically different. Nayeli, a woman from nearby Silao, spent the majority of her days at the shelter cheering up weary migrants. She wore neatly trimmed bangs that bisected her round forehead and an unwaveringly upbeat personality. "Ah, he's just missing his lady friend," she would joke with one of the male residents, cocking her head back and completing the phrase with a drawn out "haaaaaaaaa." Her two-year-old son (whom she referred to as "*el güerito*"), loved to bounce around the courtyard, kicking a ball and retrieving it in an interminably giddy game of fetch. Nayeli and the rest of the volunteers at *El Refugio* always spent their time with the migrants, not tucked away scrolling through Facebook as if they wanted nothing to do with them.

Opening the doors at *El Refugio*.

It was a particularly busy Saturday at *El Refugio*. Members of the Red Cross were visiting, as well as a group of retired American expatriates who lived in San Miguel de Allende. I arrived at the opportune moment to begin translating for the American guests. The group of ten women and one man, all sixty-plus, gathered eagerly around me, hanging on my every word. One woman would always respond with an "ahhhh" to translations such as "this is the kitchen," as if the words connoted some deep insight. Another woman had her own idiosyncratic reaction to any unwelcome news or development that I would translate. Her eyes would bulge, and her head would shoot forward and abruptly retract, as if she were gulping down a big bite of food. The group overflowed with the burning desire to help, to show off their Spanish, and to be viewed as socially active citizens. Perhaps I was not all that different from them, but I at least would not run up to three-year-old Salvadorian María, hug/strangle her, and squeak, *"Adios mi hija,"* just thirty minutes after arriving at the shelter.

As we finished our tour, the guests discharged all their burning questions. In response to one, Hugo began to emphasize the vision of the shelter, which was to create a dignified, professional, and above all safe space for all. *"Lo que pasó en el otro albergue es que la delincuencia ya está adentro."* He paused for me to translate; I hesitated, still wrapping my head around the enormity of his words. The surprise was painted lucidly across my face. *You mean the migrant shelter where I have been spending my evenings for the past eight months?* My stomach began to double over, as the eager faces awaited my translation. "What happened in the other shelter is that crime already exists inside it," I finally said awkwardly, unable to arrange the words in a coherent manner. The people around me nodded, their reactions muted compared to the cacophony of emotions brewing inside me.

Later, Hugo invited me and my sister (who was visiting to take photographs) into his office. "I'm going to tell you what I know," he expressed plainly. He began divulging his thoughts about Geoff, the director of other shelter, which I'll call "*El Albergue*." Geoff was the first person I had met there. I had wandered into his office during my initial visit, feeling slightly nervous about the place. However, nothing Geoff said during our hour-long conversation gave me reason to be wary. Indeed, he seemed very knowledgeable, and was happy to have me interview migrants in his shelter. In the coming months, however, I saw very little of him.

"You see, Geoff and I used to be friends," Hugo continued. "I owe the fact that I'm involved with migration to him." Geoff used to run another migrant shelter, Hugo explained, a precursor to *El Albergue*, which the municipal government repeatedly tried to shut down because Geoff often spoke badly of the local police and government. Hugo's involvement was designed to give the shelter a new face and shift its image for the municipal government, which seemed to work. The pair moved the shelter to its current location, changed the name, and *El Albergue* was born. It was 2013.

For a time, everything went smoothly, but soon Hugo began to note small incongruences, particularly when it came to the shelter's finances. Geoff's only job was at the shelter (which supposedly didn't pay) and his wife taught middle school. It thus seemed odd to Hugo when Geoff moved his family into a large, luxurious house, and purchased a new car. Hugo also started noticing that meat and other donations given to the shelter never seemed to make it to the migrants. But the two were friends, and ultimately, Hugo trusted Geoff.

One day, Geoff arrived at the shelter, completely distraught. Apparently, his son, who struggled with drug addiction, had stolen money from him.

"How much did he steal?" Hugo asked.

Geoff looked up at his friend. "He stole 30,000 pesos from my dresser."

Who would have 30,000 pesos just lying around their bedroom? Hugo was wary.

Geoff also seemed to be spending increasingly less time at the shelter. Often, the landlord would come by, reminding Hugo that the rent was late. Hugo would cover, claiming they didn't have the funds. But in reality, he was waiting for Geoff to pay. The shelter received some funding from the municipal government, so Hugo could not understand why they were behind on their rent and other bills. He did not want to believe that his friend was siphoning funds from a migrant shelter.

It was around this time that Hugo attended a conference on migration, with participants from various shelters around the country. Geoff was not able to attend. During one of the sessions, a speaker declared, "We don't want what happened in Celaya to happen again." What had happened in Celaya? Hugo pulled an organizer aside to inquire. "How do you not know?" the man responded. "A group of migrants were kidnapped from right outside your shelter just weeks ago."

Hugo's head was spinning. If everyone seemed to know about this crime, Geoff must as well. Why hadn't his friend told him? Each day, additional pieces of a troubling puzzle seemed to be coming together. Still, Hugo trusted his friend enough not to confront him. Years later, in the safety of his office at his new migrant shelter, he expounded, "These things (the kidnappings) happen when someone inside is involved."

Shortly after Hugo heard about the kidnapping, Geoff told him that a migrant would be coming through the shelter who was hoping to start an NGO (Non-governmental organization) in the States. The man wanted to talk to Hugo. The whole thing seemed strange. "Do you have papers?" Hugo asked this mysterious traveler; when he said no, it became clear that starting an NGO was not his true intention. This suave *depravado* then asked a nearby teenager to buy him a coke, extracting a fifty dollar bill tucked in his hair. In that moment, it was clear to Hugo that this man was in charge of the other migrants in the room. "He was a *pollero,* a *coyote,* an *enganchador,*" Hugo explained. *El Albergue* had a protocol in place for recognizing *polleros,* and keeping them out. Why had Geoff specifically invited this obvious *pollero* into the shelter? Did it mean that there were larger ties to organized crime behind him?

This was the last straw. Hugo decided to confront Geoff. To his surprise, Geoff confessed to the whole thing. "They give me cash for each migrant I hand over to them," he admitted nonchalantly. "But what else am I supposed to do? We're behind in the rent and we can't pay expenses." Hugo was sickened. The shelter was undoubtedly behind in its bills because of Geoff's lavish personal purchases, and now he was orchestrating the very abuses from which shelters are supposed to shield migrants.

Who were "they"—these corrupt characters supposedly paying Geoff for people? Hugo could not really elaborate. It was clear, however, that if someone was buying migrants, it was for one of three purposes: sex trafficking, drug trafficking, or kidnapping. These operations are not usually run by local *delicuentes* without them having some sort of tie to the cartels. Most shelter directors know the crooks around them, but do their best to keep them out because once they become entangled in the criminal world, there is no way out. Behind the shady *pollero* that Geoff invited in, there were certainly more menacing *narcos.* With these men in the picture, Hugo knew he had to get out.

Hugo immediately left his post at *El Albergue*, eventually forming *El Refugio*. According to Hugo, the environment at *El Albergue* continued to fester in toxicity. "They charge for everything there," he declared. "The first night is 'free,' but they charge fifty pesos for each additional night. And they charge for each meal, for every pair of shoes, for calls that migrants make. They get all these food and clothing donations and they charge for all of it. When a shelter starts to charge migrants," Hugo elucidated, "They begin to touch on cartel interests. When you take money away from migrants by charging them, you're actually taking away money from the cartels, since that's the money that they later steal from migrants anyway. When a shelter starts to charge, that's when you invite problems in."

It was unclear whether Geoff had started to charge migrants before or after getting involved with traffickers, as Hugo was not sure of the exact sequence of events. If Geoff charged before, perhaps he had caused the *narcos* to target the shelter by "touching on their interests." Either way, taking away migrant's money—and by Hugo's logic, the cartel's money— likely tied *El Albergue* into the ominous web of organized crime.

Hugo also alleged that kidnapping and selling migrants to *polleros* was still happening at *El Albergue*. He referenced the case of a young gay man, who had come to *El Refugio* after being kidnapped from right outside *El Albergue* and subsequently sold into sex slavery. Hugo said that he had tried to get the man to press charges, but he had refused. He had been raised Catholic, and apparently members of the church had been clients at the brothel where he was held. Priests, he stressed, had raped him. He had no desire to relive the horrendous trauma through the court process; instead, he wanted to leave it all behind.

Hugo also mentioned that he had received several death threats since he had left *El Albergue*, and he suspected Geoff was behind them. Just days before we spoke, while stopped at a light, Hugo had realized the man in the adjacent car was staring menacingly at him. The man then made a gun with his thumb and index finger and pretended to shoot him. Despite such threats, Hugo felt that he was safe. Security at *El Refugio* was tight, and he was convinced Geoff would not act on his threats (if that was indeed who they were from). "Also organized crime just has no reason to involve itself in this shelter," Hugo told me. "You have problems when you touch their interests."

I was dumbfounded. Could this all be true? I reminded myself that this was a single perspective from a man that I did not know well. Yes, his organization had the Red Cross and Oxfam behind it, but did I have any concrete reasons to trust him? Still, the oddities that I had seen at *El Albergue* seemed to confirm that, at the very least, something was going on there.

A few days later, I was combing through local news articles about immigration, when I noticed a write-up about *El Albergue*. The story celebrated the success of the shelter and the large number of people that it had aided. But one particular quote caught my eye. It was from Geoff, declaring that although the number of individuals coming through the shelter hadn't declined since Trump was elected, "the stay of each migrant (has changed), since before they stayed between forty-eight and seventy-two hours, and lately they have only been staying one day, given the fact that they prefer to continue with their journey as soon as possible." I immediately flagged this. Several migrants had told me that they were only allowed to stay overnight because of the rules, not because of some drive to get to the US a day earlier.

The ultimate question still remained: could Geoff be so corrupt as to turn migrants over to *polleros* for money? There was nothing concrete I could pinpoint to make me believe it one way or the other. However, on my last visit to *El Albergue*, I had witnessed Lupita intimidate the shelter's occupants. She had appeared at 8:00 PM to register late arrivals. Dinner was supposedly served at 7:00 PM, yet when one man asked when they would eat, Lupita erupted. "Here these ladies (my sister and I) have come to give you their time and you're being incredibly rude! You should be grateful you have this place! Food will be served when it's served."

The migrants were stunned. One of them inquired whether they could at least leave to get some food. Lupita pointed to one of the shelter rules written on a large sheet of paper, which required migrants to stay in the house after 7:00 PM. She continued in a heated tone. "That's for your own safety. We're trying to protect you. Recently there's been a white van roaming between here and Don Pulcro, trying to pick out migrants to kidnap. That's why you're not allowed to leave." Don Pulcro was a cleaning store located near the migrant shelter.

At the time, it seemed peculiar that Lupita had mentioned this so-called white van. Maybe there were things I wasn't aware of, but the neighborhood around the shelter was relatively safe, so it appeared that she was just trying to scare the migrants. After listening to Hugo's story, however, this small incident seemed to fit into what he had told me. Perpetrators often try to scare their victims when they want them to see the outside world as unsafe, and thus see their world as safe by comparison. This interaction was by no means evidence that the stories Hugo had told me about the shelter were true, but it did make me wonder and question what was really going on at *El Albergue*.

Tess and I left the shelter with a heaviness in our steps. How to digest such information? How to figure out what to do next? In the US we could have gone to the police. Here, however, there was no way to know whether the police weren't already tied up with this mess. In the US I could bring the story to a newspaper and hope they could break the story. Here, the press was not a reliable outlet, as the information was often controlled by organized crime interests. In the US, I might go to the mayor or city council. In Celaya, the local government may have already been aware, and even working in concert with *El Albergue's* purported criminal activity, given that the shelter received municipal funds.

So instead of acting promptly, I sifted through the potential consequences of acting. I was no longer going to volunteer at *El Albergue*, that much was clear. But what if Geoff found out I was visiting *El Refugio*? What if he discovered what Hugo had told me? What if the whole saga was false and Hugo was the one using me in some way? What if the detailed blog where I had been chronicling my many interviews, including the disappearance of Rosaura's husband, had been brought to the attention of the wrong folks? I tried to ignore these hypotheticals and follow a train of logical thought. Once I had examined every angle, I determined there was no reason to feel personally threatened.

It was much more emotionally daunting to deal with one raw truth: I had spent the previous eight months recording haunting stories about the journey north, only suddenly to be told that this same repulsive abuse was happening right under my nose. No longer could I compartmentalize my life from the stories that echoed in the shelter. Before, I could leave in the evening and go to dance class the next day feeling unencumbered. After my conversation with Hugo, however, my life in Celaya felt dreadfully intermingled with the darkness of migration, a world of drugs and sex trafficking and kidnappings and cartels. For eight months, I had observed this cauldron from afar in an academic manner, but now I felt its reach directly and viscerally. This core sense of despair, mixed with shock, ballooned as I realized that some of those I had interviewed may well have been handed over to traffickers. I recalled the spaces we had shared—the shelter's iron door, the battered couches, the dim lighting, the handwritten rules that littered the walls. I could see myself sitting inside this space, feeling the weight of people's words. Then, as if watching a grainy but vividly shot video, I saw myself leaving. What came next inside those spaces would never make it into my final chapter.

Fevers and Phone Calls

Two days after I spoke with Hugo, I left on vacation for Semana Santa with my sister. As our trip concluded on a Sunday evening, I peered out the bus window at the endless sweeps of fields and gangly cacti, and started to grasp that perhaps Celaya was not as safe as I had assumed. My brain pounded against my skull as a headache intensified with the penetrating blare of the sun. I decided that I would call the Fulbright Commission the next day and explain what had been relayed to me (though I still questioned if it was actually true). This was the only viable action I could come up with.

The following day, right before I planned to make the call, my temperature spiked to 103 degrees. It was no surprise given the way I felt—fluctuating between burying myself under the covers and combatting extreme heat, a pounding headache, dehydration and nausea. But I still made the call, which initially reassured me that the issue, at least in terms of my safety, was nominal. "Well you don't have to go back to the migrant shelter," my program director advised in a *what's-the-big-deal?* tone. But what about the abuses? Fulbright's main concern was me, not the allegedly corrupt corners of my host city, I was told. I then oft-handedly mentioned another instance at *El Refugio* where I had interviewed and exchanged contact information with a "migrant" that had later been identified as a *coyote*. "Careful with that one," Nayeli had warned. "The director just found out he's a *pollero* trying to swindle migrants." He was quickly booted from *El Refugio* (something I could not see happening at *El Albergue*). After mentioning this small incident on the phone, my program director added, "Let me talk to my supervisor," giving me the sinking feeling that this was not over. I waited for the next call.

Call #2 came as I lie shivering in my bed, my cheeks like hot coals, the room as stuffy as a sauna. "We are very concerned," the director of programs proclaimed. She asked for more details. She requested names and addresses. She instructed me to shut down my blog and remove any stories that discussed kidnappings in Celaya. Her questions put me back on the fear train. Should I be worried about my email? Could someone be listening to my phone calls? I waited for the next call.

In the meantime, my fever spiked, and I found the nearest hospital. "You have heat stroke," a doctor told me a few hours later, after several attempts to get an IV in my shriveled-up veins.

Call #3 came while I was hooked up to the IV, after the Fulbright personnel had spoken with the Regional Security Officer at the US Embassy. They had decided to move me to Querétaro, a notoriously safe city an hour away from Celaya. I could take over a friend's apartment, continue writing, and get oriented to the place by the other Fulbrighters who were already there. If I had to move, this was as good as an option as I might expect.

Call #4 came after I had left the hospital. "Don't make any plans in Queretaro," my program director warned. "The Secretary of Education doesn't want to put you in a new school for just a month, so we're looking into other options for where you could go." I lingered in the wretches of my dark hotel room, trying to avoid the sun and accept being in limbo.

I did not have to wait for long. As the shivering and high fever came back that evening, a second trip to the hospital ensued, where I spent another night being pumped with fluids and antibiotics. By midafternoon the next day, I received another call from the Fulbright

Commission to discuss my options. Turned out that "options" were actually "option," which was to move to Mexico City and help the Commission with administrative assistance for their summer programs. As a girl from a town of six thousand, going to a city of twenty-two million, even for a month, felt overwhelming. I pictured myself swimming in people, yet utterly alone. I said no. The Commission sent me a resignation letter to sign. I felt like I was completely giving up.

In the end, I did wind up moving to Querétaro, once the program officers decided that it was indeed okay to transfer me to a new school for a month. Logistically, it was relatively easy, but emotionally I felt uprooted and directionless. Querétaro was not Celaya, which had grown so familiar and comforting in its everyday rhythms. There was no juice man on the corner to greet me each morning; no woman at the market updating me on her family; no dance class with 14-year-old girls and forty-year-old women, all of whom adored my off-beat steps. The move had wiped away my tiny points of connection to daily life in Mexico.

My first few days at the new school exacerbated these feelings. The university had projectors in every classroom, well-organized facilities, benches, impeccable programs, and far more amenities than the previous university. But I did not know the students. No one greeted me in the halls. I ate lunch with my nose pressed into a book.

There was an uncomfortable paradox with having a safety net that could scoop me up at the first signs of "danger" there, and plop me down in a safer location. Even many of those with money in Mexico did not have that privilege. I thought about Rosaura, whose efforts to leave Guatemala City led her to Celaya, only to lose her husband. Unable to continue north, she spent many ambiguous months at *El Refugio*. A few days after I packed my things in Celaya and subleased an apartment in

Querétaro, I received word that Rosaura had returned to Guatemala City. There was no one to scoop her up and make her feel safe again.

As I grappled with disconnectedness in my new city, I simultaneously wrestled with the strong prospect that every night at *El Albergue*, migrants were checking into a supposed sanctuary that was just as menacing as what lurked outside.

A girl wanders home in the author's new Querétaro neighborhood.

Mental Fluctuations

After a few weeks in Querétaro, the thoughts of organized crime grew hazy as my immediate surroundings had shifted to colorful walls rimmed by cobblestone streets where sleek women clicked down the sidewalk in their professional high heels and soft jazz music wafted through the many downtown plazas. The vibe was super *tranquilo*.

My main preoccupation became where to find the best bar open on a Monday night. I was just an hour away from Celaya, but in a different space, physically and mentally.

Yet there were still times where I would get thrown back into the hypersensitive state that had characterized my final days in Celaya. For example, the day before I had the opportunity to go back there to get my things and say goodbye to my students, I spoke to my father.

"Are you taking the bus there?" His voice crackled through the bad service and the squealing teenagers of the university around me.

"Yeah. There's no other way to get there. But I think I'll take a taxi from the bus station to school."

"Don't 'think' that. Make it your plan. Or maybe you should take an Uber. Is Uber generally safer?"

"Yeah, Uber is usually safer."

"But then you'd have to wait for it to come." He mulled it over, his detail-oriented mind going to work. "Well, take an Uber, but wait for it inside and don't talk to anyone at the bus station."

The conversation continued on in this capacity until we had every detail of my Celaya trip mapped out. He then moved on to reminding me that someone could be monitoring my email. "Nothing in writing," he warned, and I nodded in silence at the incongruity of it all. Part of me leaned toward dismissing most of his advice as over-protective parenting. Another part, however, innately understood if the Fulbright officials had been worried enough to move me to a different city, then perhaps I shouldn't be too cavalier.

I exited the bus on the busy edge of Alameda Park in downtown Celaya. A photo exhibit lined the park fence, and a sign declared that its theme was "Mexican Culture." In the unrelenting sunlight, I squinted up at a picture of several Barbie dolls tossed inside a worn cement shower next to a bottle of Herbal Essences shampoo. The connection to Mexican culture seemed dubious at best.

"Excuse me," a woman interrupted. "Do you know if there are any public restrooms around here?" An innocent enough question, but in my hyper-vigilance, I almost ignored her and kept walking. The middle-aged woman was thick with milk white skin, a young blond girl beside her. Her fluffy black hair had probably sat in old-fashioned curlers the previous night. They wore nice clothing—the girl a white dress and a cute headband complete with a bow, the older woman a red and white polka-dot blouse.

"I'm actually not sure. They might let you use the bathroom in that coffee shop over there," I responded, immediately feeling silly for being wary of them, then upset for unconsciously trusting them because they were white, well-dressed women. I silently cursed my implicit racism, and kept walking.

While there were times during my final month in Mexico when fears of organized crime flooded my thoughts, there were also times where my caution would feel unwarranted, absurd and even selfish. Living my life as if Mexico was out to get me when there were millions of other people with tangible, visible reasons to live in fear was the height of self-centered paranoia. Unlike me, these people had no invisible Fulbright arm to save them.

One night, I went to a documentary screening about the violence in Guerrero. The film followed three female activists fighting corruption and violence in the wake of the forty-three students who had disappeared in Ayotzinapa in 2014. On the screen, the activists rummaged through bones in mass graves, sites that the state government had sup-posedly already excavated for evidence. Later, they marched with oth-ers through the streets, occasionally throwing stones at the police, which would provoke gunshots in return, which resulted in the deaths of protestors. I watched as a state police officer laughed in the faces of the shouting protestors, trivializing the fact that their relatives had dis-appeared. *Pinches indios,* he said. *Damn ignorant, rural gente.* A lawyer representing the parents of the missing students was actually quoted on film calling the relatives "*indios piojosos.*" Scumbag Indians.

After the screening, the director and the three activists took the stage. The women ran an organization supporting family members of those who had "disappeared" in Querétaro, pushing for proper inves-tigations. They were still searching for their sons, daughters, husbands. One woman broke into tears as she detailed her son's disappearance. She swallowed her tears long enough to speak, and I marveled at how despite their profound loss, they still had the courage to keep kicking up dust on the matter. Did they ever wonder if, one day, they might dis-appear too?

I thought about the ludicrousness of viewing insecurity in my situ-ation, in comparison to theirs. I had found out about the *potential* kid-napping of *other* people. I had given my contact information to someone who *might* be involved in trafficking people. I had received no direct threats and no evidence that someone was targeting me. Danger is rela-tive, except in the cases where it is not. Sitting there in that auditorium, I couldn't help but feel that my weak definition of fear ignored the real patterns of violence at work in Mexico. In terms of the ladder toward safety, I stood on the top wrung. I was the one choosing to step lower—for the experience of a greater understanding of the world. And that in of itself was an enormous privilege—to be able to view insecurity as an

Citizens gather to protest government corruption in Querétaro.

adventure, a good story, and not to have to actually live it.

As I boarded my plane home to Oregon a month later, absorbing the orange dawn light as it thickened the tarmac's horizon, this privilege was a bitter, viscous paste in my mouth. Returning to a country spouting hatred toward immigrants, and leaving a country where even the shelters where people went for protection were corrupt left me with the hallow feeling that the twisted knot of migration—that sea of treachery and harrowing sacrifice—was an incomprehensible stain on the whole of humanity.

Afterword

CORRUPTION IN ALL CORNERS, I TURN TO STORIES

"There's really no such thing as the 'voiceless.' There are only the deliberately silenced, or the preferably unheard."

—Arundhati Roy

AFTER OVER A YEAR OF unanswered messages, Roberto Campos finally wrote back.

"*Buenos días o tardes.* I'm appearing after a year. I just got out of a detention center." That was all he offered in his small screen bubble.

I was sitting in my living room when I read his message, slumped over like a Christmas present under the twelve-foot-tall tree that was still up from the holidays. It was the end of January. I was curled up under a fuzzy blanket, defrosting after a day of skiing in the mountains. During our conversation a year before, Roberto had never failed to point out that I lived in a different world than him. That fact never felt as clear as during that moment, reading his Facebook message under my Christmas tree while Roberto had just been released after being locked up for a year. I picked up the phone to dial, and his answer was immediate.

Because of his class, nationality, lack of citizenship, and even his race, Roberto's options were limited. To feed his family, he had to leave them behind. To better his circumstances, he had to endure assaults, robbery and a harrowing sense of uncertainty while traveling illegally through Mexico. To pursue freedom and opportunities in the US, he had to spend a year where his freedom was taken away in an immigrant jail. Yet he did all that while still holding on to his agency, dignity, and spirit.

Roberto had always planned to write about his experiences, and I hope he still does. While he is not voiceless, his stories are often deliberately unheard in today's America. Instead, we hear voices that say that "When Mexico sends its people, they're not sending their best . . . They're bringing drugs. They're bringing crime. They're rapists." These stereotypes fester in our society, breeding a type of hatred that stomps out the humanity of people like Roberto and his fellow migrants. It's convenient to ignore their stories because it allows us to continue to pursue policies that chafe at the very core of what's moral—not just for US citizens but for dedicated and decent human beings around the world.

Ernesto.

Migrant voices are powerful, even more so when they are actually *heard*—and not just by listening, feeling distraught, and moving on. Instead, truly hearing a story's humanity enatils empathy and respect. It forces us to put ourselves in their position, and consider what we would do. It compels us to mourn the lives lost on the journey north, and in this collective remembrance, to render their suffering less invisible.

This is why I shared the stories in this book—because I wanted to add to the full and rich body of the migrant experience. I shared because the burden of calling for a more sensible, decent approach to immigration policy shouldn't just fall on immigrants—it should also fall on those who have the privilege of living a life removed from the migrant world.

Roberto's story and the stories of all those who relentlessly follow the path north should be a call to action for those of us who are lucky enough to legally reside in the United States. They should allow us to see the absurdity of attempts to deter migrants—from pushing them into the dangerous desert to cross the border, to building yet another "impenetrable" border wall. Migrants already face enormous obstacles to get to the US, risks that would deter the average American. Yet they take on these risks because the dangers of staying in their home country are greater. They choose hope over stagnation. They suffer the journey north because they feel they have no other choice. As a country, we can choose to make that journey more arduous on the theory that they won't come, or we can reimagine what US immigration can—and should—be.

For those of us who possess the privileges that many migrants lack—especially those of us who are white—the challenge is to do more than practice benevolent sympathy. Instead, if we are able to understand the web of violence that migrants endure, we will have a real stake in changing the policies that create it.

During my first interview session at *El Albergue*, I paused to chat with an old man who referred to himself as "El abuelo." He had immigrated previously, but was now back in Celaya and was volunteering at the shelter.

"Do you know Julio Verne?" he inquired. The question was out of context and the name sounded familiar, but I couldn't place it.

"*¿Veinte mil leguas de viaje submarino?*"

My mental translator didn't work fast enough for me to recognize the words.

"Well look for that book," he directed. "Migration is like the experiences they describe. It's like going deep into the ocean for the first time and realizing that there's an entire world below. A world you never even knew existed."

A few days later, I was strolling the aisles of a book fair when the name Jules Verne caught my eye. *Twenty Thousand Leagues Under the Sea.* Of course. And only then did I see that indeed I was plunging beneath the surface of something as unimaginable as life under the sea. A hushed and secret realm where information is passed on in whispers, and the crashing of ocean waves hides the turmoil underneath. But unlike the magic and beauty of the sea, this underworld is teeming with train beasts, crooked police and politicians, organized crime and deadly deserts. It is this world that people relentlessly, resiliently endure, for the chance at something better.

Thanks to the poignant stories of those who dare to speak their truth, it is my hope that this perilous world is now becoming a little more visible.

ACKNOWLEDGMENTS

A heartfelt, profound thank you to all who supported and helped me in creating this book. Above all, I am deeply indebted to those who took the risk to tell their stories and trusted me in the process. I hope their words begin to seep into our collective consciousness.

This book would not exist without the time and space to interview, research and write provided by the Fulbright Program. Thank you to the staff at *La Comisión México-Estados Unidos para el Intercambio Educativo y Cultural* (COMEXUS) for their support in this project and to the countless professors and mentors at Bowdoin College who helped me pursue this grant, especially Janice Jaffe, Laura Henry, Cindy Stocks, and Kate Myall.

Fernanda Perez, Uzziel Velázquez Guzmán and Otty Velázquez Guzmán were my main support system during my time in Celaya. Thank you for making me feel the warmth of home hundreds of miles away and for helping me fall in love with Mexico.

Bruslee Oliván Domínguez at the Universidad Tecnológica Laja Bajío was a strong source of guidance during my time as an English Teaching Assistant. Thank you for helping me thrive and for always being a fierce advocate for students.

Tess Freeman made this book come to life. Her boundless talent for visually capturing each person's humanity adds layers and nuance far beyond what words can accomplish. Thank you for being my playmate, collaborator and rock for six weeks in Celaya—for shepherding me to hospitals and somehow making me laugh in the process. And thank you for the many hours spent on website design, title brainstorming, social media and promotion. As always, thank you for being my other half.

Robert Lasner of IG Publishing took a chance on a twenty-five-year-old first-time author and poured countless hours into shaping this book. Thank you for your careful edits and clear answers to my many publishing questions, and for tightening this book into what it is now. Thanks also to Elizabeth Clementson of IG Publishing for her support in the process. Many folks also offered advice and encouragement in the publishing process, particularly Janice Jaffe, Mathew Klingle, Allen Wells, and Kevin Sullivan.

Katherine Churchill and Caroline Martinez read over early drafts and offered thoughtful comments and critiques. I am extremely lucky to have such wonderful friends. And of course a big thank you to Roger Freeman, who did a detailed edit of the entire manuscript just two weeks before deadline and was there at a moment's notice to advise on literally every step. Thank you for pouring yourself into the process. and for your relentless love and support. Our bond only grows.

AO Forbes and Dan Pittz of Colorado Rocky Mountain School believed in this project before I knew how it would make it into the hands of readers and provided the first platform to share my work. Thank you for helping me see the impacts these stories can have on US students.

To my family, both near and afar, I am so grateful for your love and support. Dave Freeman helped me with marketing connections, Roger

Freeman helped with contract and marketing advice, and Marianne Freeman was the top admirer of my early blog interviews. Theresa Olander is my unyielding source of love and encouragement—our coffee chats always make me feel capable and inspired. Thank you for advocating for the education that brought me to this point and for your support at every turn.

Thank you to my friend-family house: Fiona Noonan, Mike Spellacy, Henry Daniels-Koch and Tess Freeman. There is nothing better than laughing with you all after a long day. Thank you to my Bend friends, who keep me goofy and help celebrate the successes, and to Lucy Skinner and Tess Hamilton for their unwavering encouragement even from afar.

Henry Daniels-Koch kept me grounded throughout the process— from scraping together all his days off to visit me in Celaya, to reminding me of my goals when worry took hold. Thank you for being your inquisitive, caring, wonderful self over these four years. I count myself so lucky to spend my days with you.

I am fortunate enough to be surrounded by thoughtful, dedicated people who work tirelessly to bring hope in times of tragedy and beauty to despair. You keep me inspired.

NOTES

PART I:

1. Jeff Ernst, Elisabeth Malkin, and Paulina Villegas, "A New Migrant Caravan Forms, and Old Battle Lines Harden," *New York Times,* January 13, 2019, https://www.nytimes.com/2019/01/13/world/americas/migrant-caravan-honduras.html.

CHAPTER ONE:

1. Jason De León, *The Land of Open Graves* (Oakland, California: University of California Press, 2015), 103.

2. U.S. Immigration and Customs Enforcement, "Deportation of Aliens Claiming U.S.-Born Children, Second Half, CY 2017," U.S. Department of Homeland Security, June 26, 2018, https://www.dhs.gov/sites/default/files/publications/ICE%20%20Deportation%20of%20Aliens%20Claiming%20U.S.%20-Born%20Children%20-%20Second%20Half%2C%20CY%20 2017.pdf; U.S. Immigration and Customs Enforcement, "Deportation of Aliens Claiming U.S. Born Children, First Half, Calendar Year 2017," U.S. Department of Homeland Security, October 12, 2017, https://www.dhs.gov/sites/default/files/publications/ICE%20%20Deportation%20of%20 Aliens%20Claiming%20U.S.%20-Born%20Children%20-%20First%20 Half%2C%20CY%202017.pdf.

3. Guillermo Cantor, "Thousands of U.S.-Citizen Children Separated From Parents, ICE Records Show," *Immigration Impact,* June 26, 2014, http://immigrationimpact.com/2014/06/26/thousands-of-u-s-citizen-children-separated-from-parents-ice-records-show/.

4. Stated during final presidential debate of the 2016 election. October 19, 2016.

5. Tal Kopan, "How Trump Changed the Rules to Arrest More Non-Criminal Immigrants," *CNN,* March 2, 2018, https://www.cnn.com/2018/03/02/politics/ice-immigration-deportations/index.html.

6. Transactional Records Access Clearinghouse, "ICE Focus Shifts Away from Detaining Serious Criminals, Sept 2016 vs Dec 2018," Syracuse University, June 25, 2019, https://trac.syr.edu/immigration/reports/564/.

7. Transactional Records Access Clearinghouse, "ICE Focus Shifts Away from Detaining Serious Criminals."

8. Tal Kopan, "Trump's Executive Orders Dramatically Expand Power of Immigration Officers," CNN, January 28, 2017, https://www.cnn.com/2017/01/28/politics/donald-trump-immigration-detention-deportations-enforcement/index.html.

CHAPTER TWO

1. Ioan Grillo, *El Narco: Inside Mexico's Criminal Insurgency* (New York: Bloomsbury Press, 2011).

2. Jerry Langton, *Gangland: The Rise of the Mexican Drug Cartels from El Paso to Vancouver* (Mississauga, Ontario: John Wiley & Sons, 2012).

3. Ioan Grillo, "Special Report: Mexico's Zetas Rewrite Drug War in Blood," *Reuters*, May 23, 2012, https://www.reuters.com/article/us-mexico-drugs-zetas-idUSBRE84M0LT20120523.

4. Ioan Grillo, *El Narco*.

5. William Finnegan, "Silver or Lead: The Drug Cartel La Familia Gives Local Officials a Choice: Take a Bribe or Bullet," *The New Yorker*, May 24, 2010, https://www.newyorker.com/magazine/2010/05/31/silver-or-lead.

6. Ioan Grillo, *El Narco*.

7. Jerry Langton, *Gangland*, 144.

8. Ioan Grillo, *El Narco*.

9. La Redacción, "¿Qué Quieren de Nosotros?" *El Diario de Juárez*, September 19, 2010. http://diario.mx/Local/2010-09-19_cfaade06/_que-quieren-de-nosotros?/.

10. Ioan Grillo, *El Narco*.

11. Ibid.

12. Marc Lacey, "Mexican Candidate for Governor Is Assassinated," *New York Times*, June 28, 2010, https://www.nytimes.com/2010/06/29/world/americas/29mexico.html.

13. Ioan Grillo, *El Narco*, 220.

14. Azam Ahmed, "In Mexico, 'It's Easy to Kill a Journalist.'" *New York Times*, April 29, 2017, https://www.nytimes.com/2017/04/29/world/americas/veracruz-mexico-reporters-killed.html.

15. Committee to Protect Journalists, "CPJ's Database of Attacks on the Press," Accessed August 15, 2019, https://cpj.org/data/killed/americas/

mexico/?status=Killed&motiveConfirmed%5B%5D=Confirmed &type%5B%5D=Journalist&cc_fips%5B%5D=MX&start_year=2017&end_year=2019&group_by=location.

16. Azam Ahmed, "Flow of Central American Children Headed to U.S. Shifts but Doesn't Slow," *New York Times*, October 6, 2015, https://www.nytimes.com/2015/10/07/world/americas/honduras-el-salvador-guatemala-mexico-us-child-migrants.html.

17. Miriam Jordan, "More Migrants Are Crossing the Border This Year. What's Changed?" *New York Times*, March 5, 2019, https://www.nytimes.com/2019/03/05/us/crossing-the-border-statistics.html.

18. La Redacción, "'Imperios de La Extorsión' Están En Honduras y El Salvador," *Diario La Prensa*, June 30, 2015, http://www.laprensa.hn/honduras/854572-410/imperios-de-la-extorsión-están-en-honduras-y-el-salvador.

19. Ioan Grillo, *El Narco*.

CHAPTER THREE:

1. "Minimum Wages around the World in English and National Languages," Wage Indicator, 2019, https://wageindicator.org/main/salary/minimum-wage.

2. "The Zapatista Struggle," *Multinational Monitor*, 1995, https://www.multinationalmonitor.org/hyper/issues/1995/04/mm0495_07.html

3. Tanya Maria Golash-Boza, *Deported: Immigrant Policing, Disposable Labor and Global Capitalism* (New York: NYU Press, 2015).

CHAPTER FOUR:

1. Jeanne Batalova, Jessica Bolter, and Allison O'Connor, "Central American Immigrants in the United States," migrationpolicy.org, August 12, 2019, https://www.migrationpolicy.org/article/central-american-immigrants-united-states.

2. Jeanne Batalova and Jie Zong, "Mexican Immigrants in the United States," migrationpolicy.org, October 11, 2018, https://www.migrationpolicy.org/article/mexican-immigrants-united-states.

3. Economic Policy Institute, "The H-2A Farm Guestworker Program Is Expanding Rapidly," *Working Economics Blog*, April 13, 2017, https://www.epi.org/blog/h-2a-farm-guestworker-program-expanding-rapidly/.

4. Drew Desilver, "No U.S. Industry Employs Mostly Immigrant Workers," *Pew Research Center* (blog), March 16, 2017, https://www.pewresearch.org/fact-tank/2017/03/16/immigrants-dont-make-up-a-majority-of-workers-in-any-u-s-industry/.

5. U.S. Green Card Office, "Diversity Immigrant Visa (DV Lottery) Qualified Green Card Countries 2019 (DV-2020 & DV-2021)," 2019, https://www.usgreencardoffice.com/qualifying-countries.

6. Phillip Connor, "US Diversity Visa Lottery Saw Near-Record Number of Applicants in 2017," *Pew Research Center* (blog), August 23, 2018, https://www.pewresearch.org/fact-tank/2018/08/23/applications-for-u-s-visa-lottery-more-than-doubled-since-2007/.

7. Kevin R. Johnson, "The Intersection of Race and Class in US Immigration Law and Enforcement," *Law and Contemporary Problems* 72, no. 4 (2009): 1–35.

8. United States Department of State, "Annual Report of Immigrant Visa Applicants in the Family-Sponsored and Employment-Based Preferences Registered at the National Visa Center as of November 1, 2018," November 1, 2018, https://travel.state.gov/content/dam/visas/Statistics/Immigrant-Statistics/WaitingList/WaitingListItem_2018.pdf.

9. United States Department of State, "Annual Report of Immigrant Visa Applicants."

10. United States Department of State, "Immigrant Numbers of March 2019," Visa Bulletin, Washington D.C.: United States Department of State, Bureau of Consular Affairs, April 2019, https://travel.state.gov/content/dam/visas/Bulletins/visabulletin_march2019.pdf.

11. United States Department of State. "Annual Report of Immigrant Visa Applicants."

12. "One Year After the SCOTUS Ruling: Understanding the Muslim Ban and How We'll Keep Fighting It," National Immigration Law Center, June 2019, https://www.nilc.org/wp-content/uploads/2019/06/Impacts-of-the-Muslim-Ban-2019.pdf.

13. Richard A. Boswell, "Racism and U.S. Immigration Law: Prospects for Reform after 9/11," *Journal of Gender, Race and Justice* 7 (2003): 325.

14. Ian Haney Lopez, *White by Law: The Legal Construction of Race* (New York: NYU Press, 1997), 27.

15. Richard A. Boswell, "Racism and U.S. Immigration Law," 326.

16. UCLA Labor Center, "The Bracero Program." UCLA Labor Center, 2014, https://www.labor.ucla.edu/what-we-do/research-tools/the-bracero-program/.

17. Richard A. Boswell, "Racism and U.S. Immigration Law," 326.

18. See United States Department of State, "Annual Report of Immigrant Visa Applicants."

19. Michael D. Shear and Julie Hirschfeld Davis, "Stoking Fears, Trump

Defied Bureaucracy to Advance Immigration Agenda," *New York Times,* December 23, 2017, https://www.nytimes.com/2017/12/23/us/politics/trump-immigration.html.

20. Scott Horsley, "FACT CHECK: President Trump's False Claims On Migrant Caravan, Tax Cuts," National Public Radio, October 23, 2018, https://www.npr.org/2018/10/23/659917659/fact-check-president-trumps-false-claims-on-migrant-caravan-tax-cuts.

21. Amber Phillips, "'They're Rapists.' President Trump's Campaign Launch Speech Two Years Later, Annotated," *Washington Post,* June 16, 2017, https://www.washingtonpost.com/news/the-fix/wp/2017/06/16/theyre-rapists-presidents-trump-campaign-launch-speech-two-years-later-annotated/; Donald Trump, "Remarks by President Trump on the Illegal Immigration Crisis and Border Security," The White House, November 1, 2018, https://www.whitehouse.gov/briefings-statements/remarks-president-trump-illegal-immigration-crisis-border-security/.

22. Josh Dawsey, "Trump Derides Protections for Immigrants from 'Shithole' Countries," *Washington Post,* January 12, 2018, https://www.washingtonpost.com/politics/trump-attacks-protections-for-immigrants-from-shithole-countries-in-oval-office-meeting/2018/01/11/bfc0725c-f711-11e7-91af-31ac729add94_story.html.

23. Josh Dawsey, "Trump Derides Protections for Immigrants from 'Shithole' Countries," *Washington Post,* January 12, 2018, https://www.washingtonpost.com/politics/trump-attacks-protections-for-immigrants-from-shithole-countries-in-oval-office-meeting/2018/01/11/bfc0725c-f711-11e7-91af-31ac729add94_story.html.

24. U.S. Citizenship and Immigration Services, "Temporary Protected Status," USCIS, November 1, 2019, https://www.uscis.gov/humanitarian/temporary-protected-status.

25. Jayashri Srikantiah and Shirin Sinnar, "White Nationalism as Immigration Policy," *Stanford Law Review,* 2019 Immigration Symposium, 71, March 11, 2019, https://www.stanfordlawreview.org/online/white-nationalism-as-immigration-policy/.

26. "One Year After the SCOTUS Ruling: Understanding the Muslim Ban and How We'll Keep Fighting It," National Immigration Law Center, June 2019, https://www.nilc.org/wp-content/uploads/2019/06/Impacts-of-the-Muslim-Ban-2019.pdf.

27. Jacey Fortin, "'Huddled Masses' in Statue of Liberty Poem Are European, Trump Official Says," *New York Times,* August 14, 2019, https://www.nytimes.com/2019/08/14/us/cuccinelli-statue-liberty-poem.html.

28. "President Donald J. Trump Is Ensuring Non-Citizens Do Not Abuse Our Nation's Public Benefit," The White House, August 12, 2019, https://www.whitehouse.gov/briefings-statements/president-donald-j-trump-ensuring-non-citizens-not-abuse-nations-public-benefit/.

29. Kevin R. Johnson, "The Intersection of Race and Class in US Immigration Law and Enforcement," Law and Contemporary Problems 72, no. 4 (2009): 1–35.

30. Richard A. Boswell, "Racism and U.S. Immigration Law," 340.

31. James R. Edwards, "Public Charge Doctrine: A Fundamental Principle of American Immigration Policy," 2001, https://cis.org/Public-Charge-Doctrine-Fundamental-Principle-American-Immigration-Policy.

32. James R. Edwards, "Public Charge Doctrine."

33. National Immigration Law Center, "Changes to 'Public Charge' Instructions in the U.S. State Department's Manual," National Immigration Law Center, February 8, 2018, https://www.nilc.org/issues/economic-support/public-charge-changes-to-fam/.

34. "State Department Visa Refusals in FY 2018 for Immigrants and Nonimmigrants," NFAP Policy Brief, National Foundation for American Policy, March 2019, https://nfap.com/wp-content/uploads/2019/03/State-Department-Visa-Refusals-In-FY-2018.NFAP-Policy-Brief.March-2019.pdf.

35. "State Department Visa Refusals in FY 2018 for Immigrants and Nonimmigrants," NFAP Policy Brief.

36. "Public Charge," Immigrant Legal Resource Center, August 2019, https://www.ilrc.org/public-charge.

CHAPTER FIVE:

1. Jan-Albert Hootsen, "Committee to Protect Journalists," On the Front Lines of Reporting in Guerrero, Mexico's Most Violent State (blog), September 11, 2017, https://cpj.org/blog/2017/09/on-the-front-lines-of-reporting-in-guerrero-mexico.php.

2. Transactional Records Access Clearinghouse, "Asylum Decisions by Custody, Representation, Nationality, Location, Month and Year, Outcome and More," Syracuse University, 2019, https://trac.syr.edu/phptools/immigration/asylum/.

3. U.S. Department of Homeland Security, "Refugees and Asylees," Department of Homeland Security, April 5, 2016, https://www.dhs.gov/immigration-statistics/refugees-asylees.

4. Patrick Michels, and Chris Vogel, "Asylum Denied: Only a Fraction of Mexicans Get U.S. Asylum," Westword, August 26, 2010, http://www

.westword.com/news/asylum-denied-only-a-fraction-of-mexicans-get-us-asylum-5109602.

5. Jaya Ramji-Nogales, Andrew Schoenholtz, and Philip Schrag, "Refugee Roulette: Disparities in Asylum Adjudication," SSRN Scholarly Paper, Rochester, NY: Social Science Research Network, May 31, 2007, https://papers.ssrn.com/abstract=983946.

6. Mica Rosenburg, Reade Levinson, and Ryan McNeill, "For U.S. Asylum Seekers, Some Judges Are a Better Bet than Others," Reuters, October 17, 2017, http://www.reuters.com/investigates/special-report/usa-immigration-asylum/.

7. Donald Trump Twitter post, November 2018, https://twitter.com/realdonaldtrump/status/1064245710747590657

8. Caroline Kelly, "Trump Belittles Democrats, Asylum Seekers in Republican Jewish Coalition Speech," CNN, April 7, 2019, https://www.cnn.com/2019/04/06/politics/trump-jewish-coalition/index.html.

9. "FACT CHECK: Asylum Seekers Regularly Attend Immigration Court Hearings," Human Rights First, January 25, 2019, https://www.humanrightsfirst.org/resource/fact-check-asylum-seekers-regularly-attend-immigration-court-hearings.

10. "Crossing the Line: U.S. Border Agents Illegally Reject Asylum Seekers," Human Rights First, May 2017, https://www.humanrightsfirst.org/sites/default/files/hrf-crossing-the-line-report.pdf.

11. Human Rights First, "Crossing the Line."

12. Matter of A-B-, Respondent, 27 I&N Dec. 316 (United States Department of Justice, Office of the Attorney General June 11, 2018).

13. Kristina Cook, Mica Rosenburg, and Reade Levinson, "Exclusive: U.S. Migrant Policy Sends Thousands of Children, Including Babies, Back to Mexico," Reuters, October 11, 2019, https://www.reuters.com/article/us-usa-immigration-babies-exclusive/exclusive-u-s-migrant-policy-sends-thousands-of-babies-and-toddlers-back-to-mexico-idUSKBN1WQ1H1.

14. Alyssa Isidoriday, Eleanor Acer, Kennji Kizuka, and Victoria Rossi, "Delivered to Danger: Illegal Remain in Mexico Policy Imperils Asylum Seekers' Loves and Denies Due Process," Human Rights First, August 2019, https://www.humanrightsfirst.org/sites/default/files/Delivered-to-Danger-August-2019%20.pdf.

15. Ibid.

16. United Nations High Commissioner for Refugees, "Advisory Opinion on the Extraterritorial Application of Non-Refoulement Obligations under the 1951 Convention Relating to the Status of Refugees and Its 1967 Protocol*," January 26, 2007, https://www.unhcr.org/4d9486929.pdf.

17. U.S. Citizenship and Immigration Services, "Policy Memorandum: Guidance for Implementing Section 235(b)(2)(C) of the Immigration and Nationality Act and the Migrant Protection Protocols," U.S. Department of Homeland Security, January 28, 2019, https://www.uscis.gov/sites/default/files/USCIS/Laws/Memoranda/2019/2019-01-28-Guidance-for-Implementing-Section-35-b-2-C-INA.pdf.

18. Maria Sacchetti and Nick Miroff, "As Trump Administration Pushes to Return More Migrants to Mexico, Legal Battle over Policy Intensifies," *Washington Post*, June 20, 2019, https://www.washingtonpost.com/immigration/as-trump-administration-pushes-to-return-more-migrants-to-mexico-legal-battle-over-policy-intensifies/2019/06/20/a486829a-92b7-11e9-b570-6416efdc0803_story.html.

19. Kristina Cook, Mica Rosenburg, and Reade Levinson, "Exclusive: U.S. Migrant Policy Sends Thousands."

20. The World Bank, "Intentional Homicides (per 100,000 People) | Data," 2019, https://data.worldbank.org/indicator/VC.IHR.PSRC.P5?view=map.

21. Seung Min Kim, Kevin Sieff, and Abigal Hauslohner, "Trump Says He Has Agreement with Guatemala to Help Stem Flow of Migrants at the Border," *Washington Post*, July 26, 2019, https://www.washingtonpost.com/politics/trump-says-he-he-has-agreement-with-guatemala-to-help-stem-flow-of-migrants-at-the-border/2019/07/26/23bf0cba-afe3-11e9-b071-94a3f4d59021_story.html.

22. Human Rights First, "Is Mexico Safe for Refugees and Asylum Seekers?" *Human Rights First*, November 2018, https://www.humanrightsfirst.org/resource/mexico-safe-refugees-and-asylum-seekers.

23. Mary Beth Sheridan, "As Trump Tightens the U.S. Border, Asylum Applicants Seek Refuge in Mexico, Elsewhere," *Washington Post*, September 8, 2019, https://www.washingtonpost.com/world/the_americas/as-trump-tightens-the-us-border-asylum-applicants-seek-refuge-in-mexico-elsewhere/2019/09/08/9cd714e6-ca67-11e9-9615-8f1a32962e04_story.html.

24. American Immigration Council, "Asylum in the United States," August 2016, http://www.nnirr.org/drupal/sites/default/files/asylum_in_the_united_states_.pdf.

25. Denise Lu and Derek Watkins, "Court Backlog May Prove Bigger Barrier for Migrants Than Any Wall," *New York Times*, January 24, 2019, https://www.nytimes.com/interactive/2019/01/24/us/migrants-border-immigration-court.html.

26. American Immigration Council, "Asylum in the United States,"

August 2016, http://www.nnirr.org/drupal/sites/default/files/asylum_in_the_united_states_.pdf.

27. "Mexican and Central American Asylum and Credible Fear Claims: Background and Context," American Immigration Council, May 21, 2014, https://www.americanimmigrationcouncil.org/research/mexican-and-central-american-asylum-and-credible-fear-claims-background-and-context.

28. "Mexican and Central American Asylum and Credible Fear Claims: Background and Context," American Immigration Council, May 21, 2014.

CHAPTER SEVEN:

1. Wayne Cornelius, Scott Borger, Adam Sawyer, David Keyes, Clare Appleby, Kirsten Parks, Gabriel Lozada, and Jonathan Hickens, "Controlling Unauthorized Immigration from Mexico: The Failure of 'Prevention through Deterrence' and the need for Comprehensive Reform," Immigration Policy Center, 2008; Jason De León, *The Land of Open Graves* (Oakland, California: University of California Press, 2015).

2. See Lauren Markham, *The Faraway Brothers: To Young Migrants and the Making of an American Life* (New York: Crown Publishing Group, 2017).

3. Óscar Martínez, *The Beast: Riding the Rails and Dodging Narcos on the Migrant Trail*, trans. by Daniela Maria Ugaz and John Washington (New York: Verso, 2014), 132.

4. Ibid, 134.

5. Simón Pedro Izcara Palacios, "Los polleros que engañan a los migrantes: norma o excepción," *Convergencia* 24, no. 74 (September 21, 2016): 13–38.

6. Jason De León, *The Land of Open Graves* (Oakland, California: University of California Press, 2015).

CHAPTER EIGHT:

1. Óscar Martínez, "Los secuestros que no importan," *El Faro*, 2008, https://www.elfaro.net/templates/elfaro/migracion/default.php?nota=noticias001.

2. Óscar Martínez, *The Beast: Riding the Rails and Dodging Narcos on the Migrant Trail*, trans. by Daniela Maria Ugaz and John Washington (New York: Verso, 2014), 96.

3. "¿Por qué en México proliferan el secuestro y la extorsión?" *Insight Crime*, November 20, 2015, https://es.insightcrime.org/noticias/analisis/mexico-prolifera-secuestro-extorsion/.

4. Ibid.

5. Gabriel Stargardter and Simon Gardner, "A FONDO-Migrantes Están

Atrapados En Multimillonario Negocio Del Secuestro En Frontera México-EEUU," Reuters, October 13, 2014, https://lta.reuters.com/articulo/latinoamerica-delito-mexico-secuestro-idLTAKCN0I21X120141013.

6. Óscar Martínez, "Los secuestros que no importan," *El Faro*, my translation, 2008, https://www.elfaro.net/templates/elfaro/migracion/default.php?nota=noticias001.

7. Maureen Meyer, "Un Trayecto Peligroso Por México: Violaciones a Derecho Humanos En Contra de Los Migrantes En Tránsito," Washington Office on Latin America, Diciembre 2010, https://www.wola.org/sites/default/files/down.

8. Ibid.

9. Óscar Martínez, *The Beast*, 94.

10. Ximena Suárez, Andrés Díaz, José Knippen, and Maureen Meyer, "Access to Justice for Migrants in Mexico: A Right That Exists Only on the Books," Washington Office on Latin America, July 2017.

11. Ibid.

12. Ibid.

13. Óscar Martínez, *The Beast*, 94.

14. Maureen Meyer, "Un Trayecto Peligroso."

15. Ibid.

16. James Bargent, "Reports of Migrant Kidnapping in Mexico Up 1000%," March 31, 2015, http://www.insightcrime.org/news-briefs/reports-of-migrant-kidnapping-in-mexico-up-1000-percent.

17. Óscar Martínez, *The Beast*, 93.

18. James Bargent, "Reports of Migrant Kidnapping."

19. Julio Ramírez, "Repunta El Secuestro de Migrantes; Se Multiplican Por Diez Los Casos," *Excelsior*, March 30, 2015, http://www.excelsior.com.mx/nacional/2015/03/30/1016260#imagen-2.

20. James Bargent, "Reports of Migrant Kidnapping."

21. "Reporting Crimes Committed against Migrants in Mexico from Abroad," Washington Office on Latin America, April 12, 2017, https://www.wola.org/analysis/reporting-crimes-committed-migrants-mexico-abroad/.

22. Diana Higareda and Montserrat Peralta, "Cifras de secuestros de migrantes centroamericanos en México por el crimen organizado," *El Universal*, August 12, 2018, https://www.eluniversal.com.mx/nacion/sociedad/secuestros-azotan-migrantes-de-centroamerica.

23. Mike LaSusa, "Mexico Migrant Kidnappings on the Rise?" *Insight Crime*, September 14, 2016, http://www.insightcrime.org/news-briefs/mexico-migrant-kidnappings-on-the-rise.

24. Michael D. Shear, Ana Swanson, and Azam Ahmed, "Trump Calls

Off Plan to Impose Tariffs on Mexico," *New York Times,* June 7, 2019, https://www.nytimes.com/2019/06/07/us/politics/trump-tariffs-mexico.html.

25. Óscar Martínez, "Una Escena Miserable En Una Frontera Miserable," *El Faro,* September 1, 2019, https://elfaro.net/es/201909/centroamerica/23606/Una-escena-miserable-en-una-frontera-miserable.htm.

26. Óscar Martínez, "Una Escena Miserable."

27. Ibid.

28. Ibid.

CHAPTER NINE:

1. Alejandro Castillo, "Programa Frontera Sur: The Mexican Government's Faulty Immigration Policy," Council on Hemispheric Affairs, October 26, 2016. http://www.coha.org/programa-frontera-sur-the-mexican-governments-faulty-immigration-policy/.

2. Azam Ahmed. "Step by Step on a Desperate Trek by Migrants Through Mexico." *New York Times,* February 8, 2016. http://www.nytimes.com/2016/02/08/world/americas/mexico-migrants-central-america.html.

3. Alejandro Castillo, "Programa Frontera Sur."

4. Sonja Wolf, "An Assessment Study of the National Migration Institute: Towards an Accountability System for Migrant Rights in Mexico," Institute for Security and Democracy, 2014: 11. http://www.academia.edu/5421638/Wolf_Sonja_coord._An_Assessment_Study_of_the_National_Migration_Institute_Towards_an_Accountability_System_for_Migrant_Rights_in_Mexico_Executive_Summary_.

5. Deb Riechmann and Nomaan Merchant, "President Trump Threatens to Close Mexican Border as Central American Caravan Heads North," *Time,* March 29, 2019. http://time.com/5561348/trump-close-mexican-border-caravan/.

6. Maya Averbuch and Mary Beth Sheridan, "Threatened by Trump, Exhausted by Caravans, Mexico Struggles with Migrant Surge," *Washington Post,* April 5, 2019. https://www.washingtonpost.com/world/the_americas/threatened-by-trump-exhausted-by-caravans-mexico-withdraws-red-carpet/2019/04/05/20f1fb76-5630-11e9-aa83-504f086bf5d6_story.html.

7. Jose Cortez, "Tempers Fray in Mexico as New Controls Frustrate U.S.-Bound Migrant Caravan," *Reuters,* April 3, 2019, https://www.reuters.com/article/us-usa-immigration-mexico-caravan-idUSKCN1RF2U1.

8. Jason Peña, "Mexico Increases Migrant Deportations to Guatemala," *Center for Immigration Studies* (blog), September 6, 2019, https://cis.org/Pena/Mexico-Increases-Migrant-Deportations-Guatemala.

9. Sonja Wolf, "An Assessment Study," 11

10. Sonja Wolf, "An Assessment Study," 6.

11. Ibid.

12. Ibid.

13. Ibid.

14. Sonja Wolf, "An Assessment Study," 20.

15. Ibid.

16. Stephanie Leutert, "Organized Crime and Central American Migration in Mexico," Mexico Security Initiative, Robert Strauss Center for International Security and Law; Lyndon B. Johnson School of Public Affairs, The University of Texas at Austin, June 2018, https://globalinitiative.net/wp-content/uploads/2018/07/Organized-Crime-and-Central-American-Migration-in-Mexico-The-University-of-Texas-at-Austin-2018.pdf.

17. Sonja Wolf, "An Assessment Study."

18. Stephanie Leutert, "Organized Crime and Central American Migration."

19. Ximena Suárez, Andrés Díaz, José Knippen, and Maureen Meyer, "Access to Justice for Migrants in Mexico: A Right That Exists Only on the Books," Washington Office on Latin America, July 2017.

CHAPTER TEN:

1. Maureen Meyer, "Un Trayecto Peligroso Por México: Violaciones a Derecho Humanos En Contra de Los Migrantes En Tránsito," Washington Office on Latin America, Diciembre 2010, https://www.wola.org/sites/default/files/downloadable/Mexico/2010/TrayectoPeligroso.pdf.

2. Maureen Meyer, "Un Trayecto Peligroso."

3. Alyson L Dimmitt Gnam, *Mexico's Missed Opportunities to Protect Irregular Women Transmigrants: Applying a Gender Lens to Migration Law Reform*, 22, no. 3 (2013): 37; William P. Simmons and Michelle Téllez, "Sexual Violence against Migrant Women and Children," *Binational Human Rights: The U.S.-Mexico Experience*. Pennsylvania Studies in Human Rights (University of Pennsylvania Press), 2014, http://www.academia.edu/download/37659450/Simmons_and_Tellez_Sexual_Violence_against_Migrant_Women_and_Children_-_Simmons_and_Mueller_Chapter_2.pdf; Deborah Bonello and Erin Siegal McIntyre, "Is Rape the Price to Pay for Migrant Women Chasing the American Dream?" *Splinter*, September 10, 2014, https://splinternews.com/is-rape-the-price-to-pay-for-migrant-women-chasing-the-1793842446.

4. Manny Fernandez, "'You Have to Pay With Your Body': The Hidden Nightmare of Sexual Violence on the Border," *New York Times*, March 3, 2019, https://www.nytimes.com/2019/03/03/us/border-rapes-migrant-women.html.

5. Manny Fernandez, "'You Have to Pay With Your Body"; Sylvanna

Falcon, "Rape as a Weapon of War: Advancing Human Rights for Women at the US-Mexico Border," *Social Justice* 28, no. 2 (2001): 31–50.

6. Manny Fernandez, "'You Have to Pay With Your Body.'"

7. Sylvanna Falcon, "Rape as a Weapon of War."

8. Manny Fernandez and Caitlin O'Hara, "They Were Stopped at the Texas Border. Their Nightmare Had Only Just Begun," *New York Times*, November 12, 2018, https://www.nytimes.com/2018/11/12/us/rape-texas-border-immigrants-esteban-manzanares.html.

9. Matthew Haag, "Thousands of Immigrant Children Said They Were Sexually Abused in U.S. Detention Centers, Report Says," *New York Times*, February 27, 2019, https://www.nytimes.com/2019/02/27/us/immigrant-children-sexual-abuse.html.

10. Deborah Bonello and Erin Siegal McIntyre, "Is Rape the Price to Pay for Migrant Women Chasing the American Dream?" *Splinter*, September 10, 2014, https://splinternews.com/is-rape-the-price-to-pay-for-migrant-women-chasing-the-1793842446.

11. Deborah Bonello and Erin Siegal McIntyre, "Is Rape the Price to Pay."

12. Jason De León, "The Efficacy and Impact of the Alien Transfer Exit Programme: Migrant Perspectives from Nogales, Sonora, Mexico," *International Migration* 51, no. 2 (April 1, 2013): 10–23. https://doi.org/10.1111/imig.12062.

13. Gabriela Diaz and Gretchen Kuhner, "Women Migrants in Transit and Detention in Mexico," Migration Policy Institute, March 1, 2007. https://www.migrationpolicy.org/article/women-migrants-transit-and-detention-mexico; Alyson L Dimmitt Gnam, *Mexico's Missed Opportunities*; William P. Simmons and Michelle Téllez, "Sexual Violence against Migrant Women and Children"; Jason De León, "The Efficacy and Impact of the Alien Transfer Exit Programme: Migrant Perspectives from Nogales, Sonora, Mexico," *International Migration* 51, no. 2 (April 1, 2013): 10–23, https://doi.org/10.1111/imig.12062.

14. Manny Fernandez, "'You Have to Pay With Your Body.'"

CHAPTER ELEVEN:

1. Adam Edelman, "A Look at Trump's Most Outrageous Comments about Mexicans as He Attempts Damage Control by Visiting with Country's President," *New York Daily News*, August 31, 2016, https://www.nydailynews.com/news/politics/trump-outrageous-comments-mexicans-article-1.2773214.

2. Dara Lind, "Donald Trump's Appalling Reaction to a Hate Crime Committed in His Name," *Vox*, August 20, 2015, https://www.vox.com/2015/8/20/9182169/trump-hate-crime.

3. Declan Walsh, "'The Wall Is a Fantasy,'" *New York Times*, October 14,

2016, https://www.nytimes.com/2016/10/16/opinion/sunday/the-wall-is-a-fantasy.html.

4. Gregory Yee, "President Donald Trump's Immigration Ban Felt in South Carolina, Recent Clemson Graduate Taken off Flight," *The Post and Courier*, January 28, 2017, https://www.postandcourier.com/news/president-donald-trump-s-immigration-ban-felt-in-south-carolina/article_f9c09f00-e59b-11e6-b47d-273fc4f17562.html.